THE AUTHOR

Tony Gould grew up on a Devon farm. He contracted polio while serving as a National Service subaltern in the 1/7th Gurkha Rifles. After studying English at Cambridge, he worked as a BBC Radio talk and documentaries producer and as literary editor of *New Society* and, later, the *New Statesman*. His books include *In Limbo: The Story of Stanley's Rear Column* (1979), *Inside Outsider: The Life and Times of Colin MacInnes* (1983), *Death in Chile: A Memoir and a Journey* (1992), *A Summer Plague: Polio and Its Survivors* (1995), *Imperial Warriors: Britain and the Gurkhas* (1999) and *Don't Fence Me In: Leprosy in Modern Times* (2005).

Following page: a detail from an engraving taken from the portrait of Lady Susan by Francis Cotes, early 1760s.

Lady Susan's Unsuitable Marriage

Pride & Privation in Georgian England

Tony Gould

First published in 2018 by The Dovecote Press Ltd
Stanbridge, Wimborne Minster, Dorset BH21 4JD

ISBN 978-0-9955462-5-7
Text © Tony Gould
Illustrations © see Acknowledgements

Tony Gould has asserted his rights under the Copyright, Designs and Patent Act 1988 to be identified as author of this work

Typeset in Caslon and designed by Tony Garrett

Printed and bound in Singapore by KHL

All papers used by The Dovecote Press are natural, recyclable products made from wood grown in sustainable, well-managed forests.

A CIP catalogue record for this book is available from the British Library

All rights reserved

1 3 5 7 9 8 6 4 2

Contents

List of Illustrations		6
Preface		7
Part One: Elopement and Exile		15
1	A Clandestine Marriage	17
2	Merchants and Mohawks	30
Part Two: Attendance and Dependence		53
3	Stinsford	56
4	The Dye Is Cast	69
Part Three: Darby and Joan		79
5	A Dreadful Malady	80
6	Pandora's Box	88
7	Trials of a Tax Gatherer	99
Part Four: Joan Alone		119
8	The Absent One	120
9	The Restoration of a Picture	128
10	A Prodigy	135
Acknowledgements		143
Sources		144
Reference Notes		145
Select Bibliography		155
Index		157

List of Illustrations

Illustrations in the text

Frontispiece Engraving of Francis Cotes' portrait of Lady Susan.
Page 10 The Fox and Digby family trees.
Page 12 The Fox Strangways family tree.
Page 52 Map of the family lands in the West Country.
Page 129 Engraving of Francis Cotes' portrait of William O'Brien.
Page 135 Holland House, *c.*1752.
Page 142 The O'Briens' memorial tablet in Stinsford Church.

Colour illustrations between pages 64 and 65

1. *Lord Hervey and his Friends* by William Hogarth (*c.* 1742).
2. The young Stephen Fox.
3. Lady Susan by Katherine Read.
4. Lady Sarah Lennox, Charles James Fox and Lady Susan Fox-Strangways by Sir Joshua Reynolds.
5. David Garrick and his friends, engraving after Hogarth.
6. Lady Sarah as Almeria in Congreve's *The Mourning Bride*, pastel by Katherine Read.
7. Ste Fox (later, 2nd Lord Holland), pastel by Katherine Read.
8. Lady Susan Fox-Strangways aged 18, painted by Allan Ramsay.
9. Henry Thomas, 2nd Earl of Ilchester, painted by Thomas Beach in 1778.
10. Charles James Fox painted by Karl Anton Hickel in 1794.
11. Southern view of New York City from across the East River in the 1760s (New York Public Library).
12. Bernard Ratzer's *Plan of the City of New York*, 1776 (Library of Congress Geography and Map Division).
13. Johnson Hall, New York, 1772 by Edward Lamson Henry (1903).
14. Stinsford in the 21st century.
13. William O'Brien and Lady Susan in two pastels by Francis Cotes from the early 1760s.

Preface

If you step into the church at Stinsford, outside Dorchester, and walk up the aisle to the chancel you will see on your right the twin tablets of a memorial to William O'Brien and his wife, Lady Susan O'Brien, who died in 1815 and 1827 respectively. The wording on these tablets — of O'Brien: 'his amiable disposition, cultivated mind, and worthy character endeared him to all who knew him!' and of Lady Susan: 'THE FAITHFUL WIFE AND INSEPARABLE COMPANION' – made a deep and lasting impression on Stinsford's most famous son, Thomas Hardy. He would recall the occupants of Stinsford House — next door to the church in which they are buried — in the autobiography he wrote for posthumous publication (as a biography 'compiled' by his second wife Florence), as well as in a poem which he called 'The Noble Lady's Tale'.

Hardy had personal links with Lady Susan and her family through his parents and grandparents. His mother Jemima hailed from the village of Melbury Osmond, which takes its name from the big house, parts of which date from Tudor times, and 5,000-acre estate with a deer park that Susan's father, Stephen Fox, 1st Earl of Ilchester, acquired through his marriage to the heiress Elizabeth Strangways Horner. From the age of thirteen Jemima lived and worked in the household of Lady Susan's youngest brother (and my great-great-great-grandfather) the Hon. Charles Redlynch Fox-Strangways, vicar of nearby Maiden Newton, where she eventually became cook. Later on she was in service at Stinsford House itself. But that was after Lady Susan's time; the house was then occupied by the Rev Edward Murray, brother-in-law of the 3rd Lord Ilchester, who had appointed him vicar of Stinsford not long before Susan died.

Both of Hardy's grandmothers had 'seen and admired' O'Brien at Stinsford church; and his Hardy grandfather (also called Thomas, as was his father) had a closer acquaintance with the O'Briens. Not only did he erect their memorials in the church; he also built their vault — in strict accordance with Susan's instructions to 'make it just large enough for our two selves only'.

Of Lady Susan, Hardy says that his father 'when a boy chorister in the gallery of the church used to see her, an old and lonely widow, walking in the garden in a red cloak' – a poignant image which clearly appealed to the poet-novelist. Such connections 'lent the occupants of the little vault in the chancel a romantic interest in the boy's mind at an early age,' he reports (writing of himself in the third person).

In addition to whatever below-stairs gossip he may have gleaned about the O'Briens from his closest relatives and others, Hardy was well-informed about the century-and-a-half-old scandal of their unsuitable marriage. He quotes Horace Walpole's observation that he 'could not have believed that Lady Susan would have stooped so low' and goes on:

> Though in these modern days the 'stooping' might have been viewed inversely — for O'Brien, besides being *jeune premier* at Drury, was an accomplished and well-read man, whose presentations of the gay Lothario in Rowe's *Fair Penitent*, Brisk in *The Double Dealer*, Sir Harry Wildair in *The Constant Couple*, Archer in *The Beaux' Stratagem*, Sir Andrew Aguecheek, the Prince in *Henry the Fourth*, and many other leading parts, made him highly popular, and whose own plays were of considerable merit. His marriage annihilated a promising career…

'The Noble Lady's Tale' is not one of Hardy's more memorable poems. At the heart of it is the conceit that O'Brien, years after his heyday as an actor, returns to the stage at Drury Lane to give a single valedictory performance, leaving an anxious 'Lady Su' or 'Susie', who is telling the story, in 'Our grey hall' at Mellstock (Hardy's fictional name for Stinsford).

Lady Su's delight at her husband's swift return from London turns to despair when she sees the expression on his face. At her prompting, he admits that he *failed*: something had distracted him but he is reluctant to tell her what it was. When she presses him, reminding him 'How faith and frankness towards him/ Ruled me through', he repeats her words 'faith' and 'frankness', calling them 'wedded wealth', and goes on: '… *I gave such/ Liberally,/ But you, Dear, not. For you suspected me.*' He claims he had caught sight of her at the back of the auditorium and the thought that she could have had so little faith in him as to follow him to London had thrown him. She denies having ever left the house, but he insists she was there — if not in person, '*It was my wraith* — projected…/ Thither, by my tense brain at home aggrieved.' And that's what he continued to believe until the day he died and was buried in '[t]he little vault with room for one beside'.

However implausible Hardy's imagined critical moment in the O'Briens' marriage may be, it is psychologically astute. The fictional O'Brien's return to the stage at Drury Lane for just one night is a convincing metaphor for the despairing bid for freedom from dependence on handouts from Susan's mother made by the actual O'Brien when — no longer young and in defiance of Susan's wishes — he took himself off to London to study for the bar. In the long run he *failed* in that, too, suffering an almost terminal breakdown in health, that surely had as much to do with a sense of the damage he was doing to the marriage on which both he and Susan had staked everything, as with the stresses and strains of studying law at an advanced age.

Hardy's instinct takes him to the nub of the matter, the fulcrum of the marriage — of any marriage perhaps, since all marriages rest on questions of faith and frankness, 'wedded wealth'. Whether the real O'Brien would ever have accused Susan of doubting him is another matter, though her strong opposition to his belated attempt to carve out a second career for himself in court, rather than on the stage, undoubtedly contributed to his ultimate failure, since he was well aware of her scepticism about his ability to carry it off.

In 'The Noble Lady's Tale', O'Brien 'seems to waste away' after the 'unhappy event' that shakes his faith in 'Susie'. And in reality too, after his failed attempt at being a barrister, he seems to have settled increasingly for a life of valetudinarianism. It is one of what Hardy would have called life's little ironies that in doing this he came closest to fulfilling Susan's most cherished desire — that he should find satisfaction in living the life of a country gentleman — but at a greater cost than she would have wished in terms of their mutual well-being.

LADY SUSAN'S UNSUITABLE MARRIAGE

THE FOX AND DIGBY FAMILIES

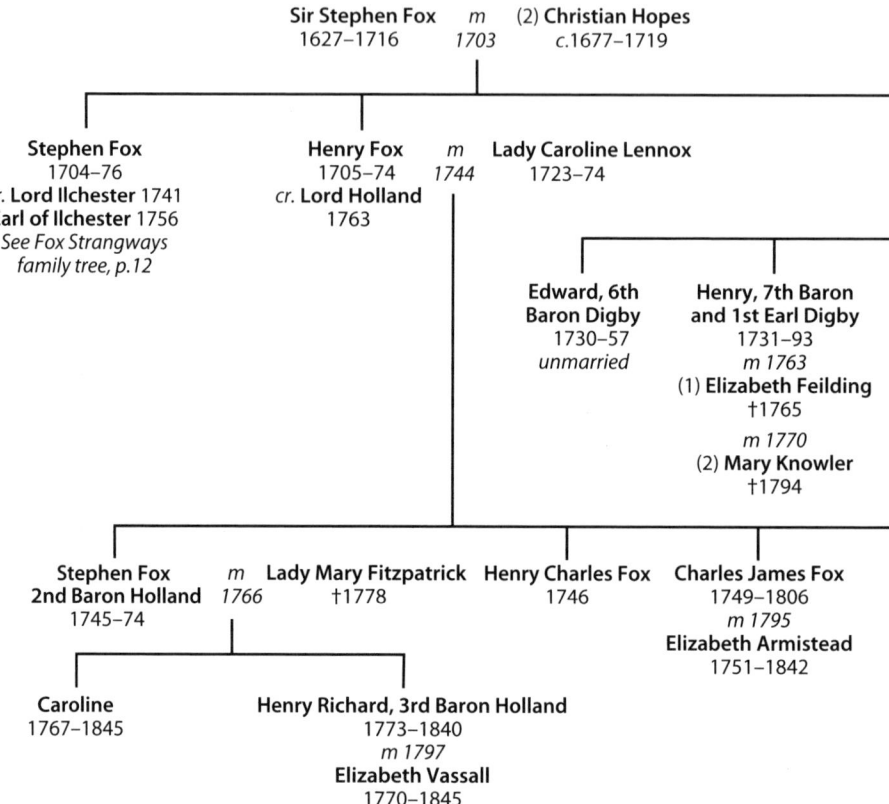

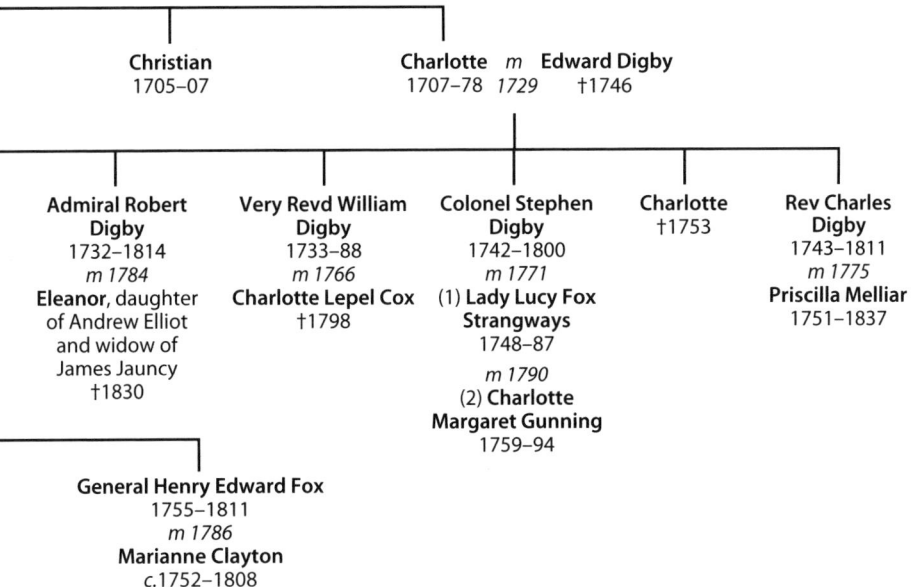

LADY SUSAN'S UNSUITABLE MARRIAGE

THE FOX STRANGWAYS FAMILY

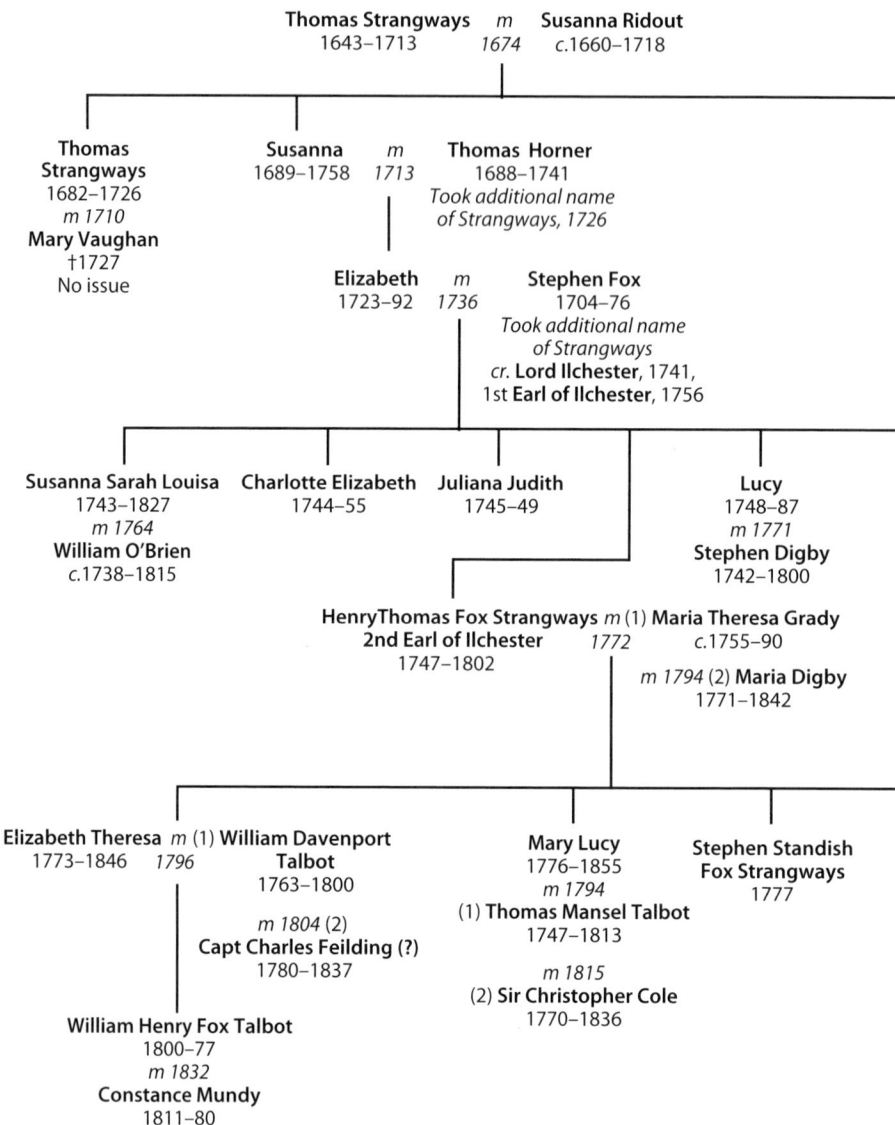

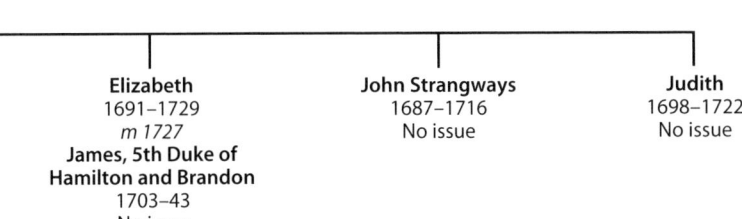

Elizabeth	John Strangways	Judith
1691–1729	1687–1716	1698–1722
m 1727	No issue	No issue
James, 5th Duke of		
Hamilton and Brandon		
1703–43		
No issue		

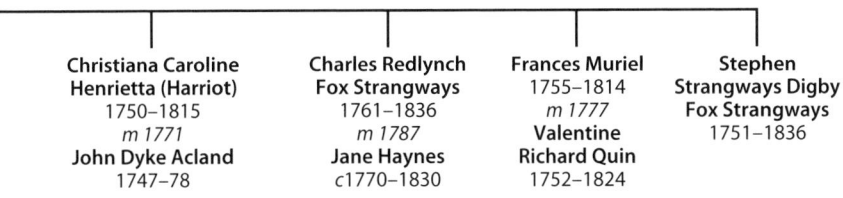

Christiana Caroline Henrietta (Harriot)	Charles Redlynch Fox Strangways	Frances Muriel	Stephen Strangways Digby Fox Strangways
1750–1815	1761–1836	1755–1814	1751–1836
m 1771	m 1787	m 1777	
John Dyke Acland	Jane Haynes	Valentine	
1747–78	c1770–1830	Richard Quin	
		1752–1824	

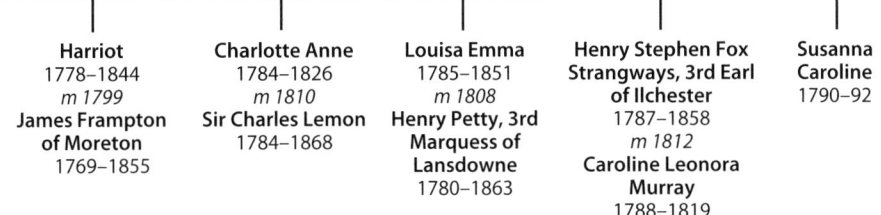

Harriot	Charlotte Anne	Louisa Emma	Henry Stephen Fox Strangways, 3rd Earl of Ilchester	Susanna Caroline
1778–1844	1784–1826	1785–1851	1787–1858	1790–92
m 1799	m 1810	m 1808	m 1812	
James Frampton of Moreton	Sir Charles Lemon	Henry Petty, 3rd Marquess of Lansdowne	Caroline Leonora Murray	
1769–1855	1784–1868	1780–1863	1788–1819	

PART ONE:
Elopement and Exile

I am distracted — I don't know what to do or what to say — I sit down ten times a day, write a sheet of paper full of incoherencies & almost madness which when I read over I throw into the fire — start up & walk ten miles in the hour in my room backwards & forwards with you in my heart, in my head, in my mouth — I am incessantly asking you if you can quite forget me? If you can, after having alternately made me the happiest & most miserable man in the world for a twelvemonth, in all which time God who only knows my heart can tell I never once have thought of any but yourself, if you can now, when I thought my happiness compleat! now learn to forget, and abandon me to the despair and wretchedness that ever will attend me if I lose you, can you forget me? can you ever? I never can forget you, not even for a moment, never shall! nor do I think that I can live without you — oh shocking idea, let me get rid of it! Yet why shou'd I endeavour to make you miserable, why persuade you to abandon father, friends, nay even the slightest of your pleasures, and for me! what merit have I, what title to such a sacrifice! what return can I make for the distress you are & have been in? for the thousand thousand wants you soon wou'd feel in being mine! nothing but love and esteem — love without decrease; a most grateful heart, that wou'd ever try to keep care from you & look upon you as my only good. But what is that? nothing! nothing for the loss of family & friends, and all those numberless elegancies that such delicacy as yours must want, and always has enjoyed — do forgive me, give me up at once — don't let me disturb the happiness and elevated joys that you was born to — let me despair and die — its no matter! I was born to be unfortunate — to know you, to have you tell me that you loved [me], to lose you — to — am I to lose you? no, I must not, can not, will not give you up. I'll do a thousand things to get money, you shall feel no wants, but what I hope I shall soon be able to atone for — can't I supply the place of father, mother? you wou'd be that, and more to me! You will be all the world to me, and what is all the world if the mind's unhappy, if we must sigh for something unpossess'd? do my heart's only joy, believe me everything you wish, and make me bless'd above all men! think me what I am, the most enamour'd, constant, sincere, frugal and everlasting lover, ever to be entirely your own, and ever the most assiduous to make you the happy woman you wou'd wish to be... don't torture me any more about any thing but the time of being yours — I can't bear the least thought of your hesitating or wavering in your opinion of me, resolve to try my truth — you will not be deceiv'd.'

— William O'Brien to Lady Susan Fox-Strangways (undated, 1763/4)

I
A Clandestine Marriage

On the morning of Saturday 7 April 1764 the twenty-one-year-old Lady Susan Fox-Strangways walked out of her father's London house at No. 31 (Old) Burlington Street, saying she was having breakfast with her closest friend Lady Sarah Bunbury (née Lennox). She was going by way of the painter Katherine Read, for whom she was sitting for her portrait. She was accompanied by a footman, but at a little distance from the house made out she had forgotten the bonnet in which she was to be drawn and sent him back to fetch it. Once on her own, Susan set off by Hackney coach in a different direction and, at a prearranged spot, met the man she had been secretly in love with for some time, a handsome and popular young Irish actor in David Garrick's Drury Lane company by the name of William O'Brien. They were married in Inigo Jones's St Paul's, Covent Garden (still known as the actors' church), and immediately afterwards left for his villa in Dunstable.

Five days later the arch-gossip of the mid-eighteenth century, Horace Walpole, breathlessly reported all this — and more — in a letter to his friend the Earl of Hertford, adding an apostrophe to the Countess: 'My Lady — my Lady Hertford! What say *you* to permitting young ladies to act plays, and go to painters by themselves?'

Walpole was a fervent admirer of the acting abilities of Lady Susan and Lady Sarah; three years earlier he had attended a performance of Nicholas Rowe's verse tragedy *Jane Shore* at Holland House — the home of Susan's uncle (and Sarah's much older brother-in-law) Henry Fox. Afterwards he had written to George Montagu, 'I was infinitely more struck by the last scene between the two women than ever I was when I have seen it on the stage. When Lady Sarah was in white with her hair about her ears and on the ground, no Magdalen by Correggio was half so lovely and expressive.' But it was one thing to participate in private theatricals and quite another to elope with an actor. For the eldest child of Stephen Fox, 1st Earl of Ilchester, who doted on Susan, to marry a penniless Irish actor was, quite simply, a calamity.

As Walpole put it to Lord Hertford, 'Even a footman were preferable.'

Walpole criticised Lord Ilchester for his 'credulity and negligence'. He informed his correspondent that the affair had been going on for at least a year and a half, during which time O'Brien had become so adept at counterfeiting Lady Sarah's handwriting that Lord Ilchester himself had unknowingly delivered some of his love letters to Susan. The family had remained in ignorance of the affair 'till about a week before the catastrophe', when Miss Read had taken another aristocratic client, Lord Cathcart, into her confidence over what she feared was going on in her studio. 'My Lord,' she had told him in a whisper, 'there is a couple in [the] next room that I am sure ought not to be together, I wish your lordship would look in.' The peer did so and straightaway informed Lord Ilchester of what he had seen. According to Walpole, 'Lady Susan was examined, flung herself at her father's feet, confessed all, vowed to break off — but — what a *but*! – desired to see the loved object, and take a last leave.'

Instead of putting her 'under lock and key in the country', as Walpole suggests he should have done, the trusting Lord Ilchester had granted her wish, thus enabling the lovers to finalise plans for their elopement — Lady Susan having just come of age — under cover of a tearful parting.

As the eldest daughter of an earl Lady Susan had been expected to make a good — i.e., dynastic — marriage that would ensure her a comfortable life, enhance her family's standing in society and, not least, set a good example to her younger siblings. For Susan's lineage was far from ancient by aristocratic standards. Her paternal grandfather, Stephen Fox, came of humble Wiltshire stock but, after loyally following Charles II during the years of his exile in France, rose to become the restored monarch's Paymaster-General and died wealthy and widely respected.

Sir Stephen, as he had become, left two sons by his second marriage (those of his first having predeceased him). Stephen and Henry Fox were both heavily influenced by the bisexual courtier Lord Hervey (butt of the poet Pope's satire in his *Epistle to Dr Arbuthnot*), under whose guidance they switched their allegiance from the Tory party to Sir Robert Walpole's Whig administration. Henry — later Lord Holland — followed a career in politics, becoming Paymaster-General to George II, just as his father had been to Charles II, also making a fortune, which would eventually be almost entirely consumed by the gambling debts of his two elder sons, Ste and Charles James Fox.

Stephen (Sir Stephen's elder son) was ennobled as Lord Ilchester (the earldom would follow later) largely through the influence of Lord Hervey, with whom he had an intimate, possibly physical, relationship over several years before his marriage. Despite his intimacy with Lord Hervey, Stephen was less interested in politics than his younger brother (to whom he gladly handed over his parliamentary seat in one of the rottenest boroughs in England, Hindon in Wiltshire, in 1735); he favoured country life — and sports — over living in London, which he visited as infrequently as he could, preferring to remain at Redlynch, near Bruton in Somerset, the manor house he had inherited from his father in which Susan spent much of her happy childhood.

Both brothers had made 'good' marriages: Stephen's to the heiress Elizabeth Strangways Horner brought the Strangways name and the vast Dorset estate of Melbury with its deer park and Tudor tower, as well as other properties, into the Fox family; and Henry's to Lady Caroline Lennox, eldest daughter of the 2nd Duke and Duchess of Richmond (who opposed it), greatly improved his social standing — though not quite so dramatically as Horace Walpole would have us believe when he writes: 'Mr Fox fell in love with Lady Caroline Lennox, asked for her, was refused and stole her. His father was a footman; her great-grandfather was a King…' Caroline was indeed the great-granddaughter of Charles II, but not in the legitimate line of succession. Her great-grandmother was his mistress Louise de Kerouaille, though her sexual services to the Merry Monarch earned her the title of Duchess of Portsmouth, just as the 'footman' Stephen Fox's financial services to the profligate King won him a knighthood.

The Duke of Richmond had been a political ally of Henry Fox, but he and the Duchess agreed with Walpole. They ostracised their daughter and Fox for many years after their marriage and insisted that Lady Caroline's younger siblings did likewise. Lady Emily Lennox, who was closest to Caroline in age, waited only until her own (approved) marriage to James, Earl of Kildare (later Duke of Leinster), freed her to resume her intimacy with her older sister. She quickly became a favourite with Henry, too, and could get away with saying whatever she liked to him. For instance, when his brother was made an earl, Emily wrote that she was glad to hear of Lord Ilchester's promotion: 'He is a sweet man worth a thousand of you, much better humoured, ten thousand times better bred, much livelier, and I believe full as clever: only that you have a cunning, black devilish countenance, and he has a cheerful, pleasant one: you are an ambitious, vain toad, and he likes to live quietly in the country.' Many a true word... Certainly, Stephen Fox had finer features than his beetle-browed and swarthy younger brother.

As the first child of either of the Fox brothers, Lady Susan Strangways (as she became known) was adored equally by her father and her uncle and grew up with an exaggerated sense of her own importance. The fact that her closest friend Lady Sarah Lennox (Lady Caroline's youngest sister) was being courted by George III when he came to the throne in 1760, and that the King used Lady Susan (herself the object of amorous advances from George's younger brother William, Duke of Gloucester) as a kind of go-between, only increased her *amour propre*. It is not surprising, then, to find that in her youth she was regarded as 'the proudest of the proud'.[1]

What is surprising is that she should have defied all expectations — and, more particularly, her family's wishes — by marrying a penniless Irish actor. Horace Walpole was not alone in wondering how Lady Susan could have 'stooped so low'. David Garrick, the actor-manager of Drury Lane who had plucked William O'Brien from the Dublin stage, wrote to the Duke of Devonshire: 'I always thought she had a foolish liking for ye Drama, & ye dramatis personae, but I could not have imagin'd, ye the flesh wd have overpower'd her Spirit, when there was a good understanding to have help'd in the struggle – 'tis a most deplorable Business indeed!'

It was certainly a deplorable business for Garrick. In the five and a half years William O'Brien had been at Drury Lane — then one of just two theatres licensed to put on plays in London[2] — he had proved a more than adequate replacement for the great Henry Woodward (who had departed to become actor-manager in Dublin). His debut on 3 October 1758, aged twenty, playing the role of Capt. Brazen in George Farquhar's *The Recruiting Officer*, drew high praise from the drama critic of the *London Chronicle*:

---

[1] Forty-six years later, staying with friends near Andover, Lady Susan met an old military man, General Sir William Medows, who remembered her from her youth and had told their hostess that she had then been 'the *haughtiest* young Lady' he had ever encountered. When apprised of this, Susan remarked that she had no recollection of the occasion, adding loftily, 'but I dare say he was troublesome'.

[2] The other was Covent Garden. A third, the Haymarket, received a royal warrant in 1767, but for the summer season and the duration of the actor-manager Samuel Foote's life only.

1 A Clandestine Marriage

The character of Brazen never existed in human nature, but is merely the child of Farquhar's own licentious invention… and for this reason I imagined it impossible for any actor to appear to advantage in it, without having recourse to that buffoonery and grimace which has always been made use of by the most eminent to support it; but I was agreeably surprised to find myself mistaken: for the young gentleman who has now got it into his possession goes through the whole with a genuine comic spirit; and, by his peculiar method of acting it, in a great measure corrects the unnatural absurdity of the writer.

The handsome young actor's London debut delighted the audience quite as much as the critics and O'Brien was off to a flying start.

In the 1758-59 season alone, he had learned fourteen other new parts and given repeat performances of most of them. These included Lucio in *Measure for Measure*, Polydore in Otway's Restoration verse tragedy *The Orphan*, Jack Meggot in *The Suspicious Husband* by Dr Benjamin Hoadly, Witwoud in Congreve's *The Way of the World* and Brisk in the same author's *The Double Dealer*, Master Stephen in Ben Jonson's *Every Man in His Humour*, Young Clackit in Garrick's *The Guardian*, as well as Daffodil in his *The Male Coquette*, Laertes in *Hamlet*, and Tom in Richard Steele's *The Conscious Lovers*. Garrick's satisfaction with his protégé is borne out by the fact that, unusually for an actor in his first season, O'Brien was granted a solo benefit on 26 April 1759, in which he'd played Lord Foppington in Colley Cibber's *The Careless Husband*.

Over the next five seasons he expanded his repertoire considerably, even working out of season in 1761, when the celebrated mimic, satirist and *enfant terrible* of eighteenth-century theatre, Samuel Foote, joined forces with the somewhat crotchety Irish ex-actor and playwright, Arthur Murphy, to take over Drury Lane for an experimental summer season, in which O'Brien played the juvenile lead Beverley in Murphy's marital comedy, *All in the Wrong*.

Garrick's contemporary biographer, Thomas Davies, says of O'Brien: 'In elegance of deportment, and variety of graceful action, he excelled all the players of his time.' Writing during O'Brien's lifetime, Davies is at pains to avoid naming him, referring to him only as an 'accomplished young gentleman, whose family connections have long since, to the great regret of the public, occasioned his total separation from the stage'. The nineteenth–century theatre historian John Genest has no such qualms and censures O'Brien for his readiness to 'sink the player' in accordance with the wishes of his wife's family 'and to bury in oblivion those years of his life which are the most worth being remembered'.

Small wonder, then, that Garrick should disapprove of a marriage that deprived him of such a treasure.

In the mid-eighteenth century, Drury Lane and Covent Garden held a tremendous allure for young aristocrats like Lady Susan and Lady Sarah — along with the even younger Charles James Fox. On 24 October 1761, Sarah wrote a long letter to Susan at Redlynch, adding a PS: 'Oh Lord! only think, I had almost forgot the most important thing…' This was that Charles, who had only recently gone to Eton, had been highly commended for Latin verses proclaiming his undying love for Susan. 'There now,' Sarah concluded, 'are you not proud, to have your name wrote in a scholar's exercise?'

As precocious in love as he was in Latin verse, the not-yet-thirteen-year-old Charles couches one of his poems in the form of a dialogue with a cousin on the merits of their respective *inamoratas* – 'Celia' (Susan) and 'Stella' (Sarah). Fox does not attempt to win the argument by drawing attention to Celia's physical attributes; he scorns such a skin-deep approach to beauty and expresses his preference in terms of personality — for Celia's 'fire' over Stella's 'gentleness'. But Susan, six years older than her cousin and already smitten with another, did not reciprocate Charles's puppy love, however flattering she may have found such devotion. When he discovered this, Charles refused to believe that Susan could possibly have chosen someone other than him — so convinced was he of the irresistibility of his charms. He repeatedly expressed his bafflement to Sarah.

At about this time, the three of them were painted together in a group portrait at Holland House by Joshua Reynolds (*see colour plates*). Susan and Charles are standing in the garden while Sarah leans out of a casement above their heads, stretching an arm towards a bird Susan is cradling in her hand and holding up to her. Susan loathed this picture, though she acknowledged that it was a 'spirited good likeness' of Charles. What she objected to — as she would write to her eldest niece Lady Elizabeth Feilding half a century later — was Reynolds's representation of Sarah and her: 'Lady Sarah & I were disfigured & insipid (which we were not).' She has a point. While Sarah appears quite elegant, Susan looks overweight (which she may have been), even frumpish, with bulgy eyes; both of them lack the freshness of youth.

There are other, more fetching portraits of Susan. Charles Fox considered the best likeness, with its teasing smile, was the one by Katherine Read (whose studio she'd found so convenient a place for trysts with O'Brien before Miss Read shopped her to Lord Cathcart).

Susan, still languishing in her father's house at Redlynch, missed the Holland House theatricals over the Christmas and New Year period of 1761/62. But Sarah faithfully reported to her all that was going on, including how disagreeable Charles was being: 'he won't learn his part perfect, won't rehearse, in short shews plainly that your not being here is the reason he won't enter in to it…' But Charles must have got over his sulks. A fortnight later, Henry Fox proudly informed his brother that Charles, in the role of Zanga, 'a captive Moor' intent on vengeance over his Spanish captors in *The Revenge* by Edward Young (better known for his long poem, *The Complaint: or Night Thoughts on Life, Death, and Immortality*), 'will act [the part] shockingly well'.

Henry Fox was a notoriously indulgent parent, or (in the case of Susan and Sarah) surrogate parent; he believed young people could do no wrong and the more precocious they were, the better it pleased him. It delighted him, for instance, when a pert young Susan remarked that if she were the King she would every so often do something startling, just to keep the politicians on their toes. Later in life, Lady Susan would be highly critical of her uncle's permissiveness, recording in her journal in 1818, after a visit to her oldest and dearest friend, that Lady Sarah had agreed with her 'in thinking that no young person could be with my Uncle Holland without being the worse for it — his excessive praises & flattery excited our vanity, made us enemies & unfitted us for any society that was not *superfine*'. But at the time she basked in his adoration and adored him in return.

Stage and star struck, believing in her own invulnerability and encouraged by the younger Sarah, she set about seducing the handsome young actor who was the eighteenth-century equivalent of a matinée idol. O'Brien turned out to be a willing accomplice in this dangerous game, playing the adoring swain to perfection and colluding in Susan's outrageous plan to overturn both social and sexual norms. While it might be acceptable for a gentleman to pick up an actress and keep her as a mistress, it was unheard of for a woman of rank and fashion to pay court to an actor — let alone marry one. No wonder her father, when he finally got wind of the romance that was flourishing in the heady atmosphere of Drury Lane and Holland House, moved swiftly to scotch it.

But by then it was too late. Susan had turned twenty-one in February 1764 and — unlike her sovereign, who had forsworn love in favour of duty by marrying a dowdy German princess instead of the beautiful Lady Sarah — was free (legally, at least) to follow the dictates of her heart, though in doing so she was far from free of foreboding.

On the eve of her wedding, she wrote an uncharacteristically incoherent letter to her Uncle Henry, now Lord Holland, the gist of which was how dearly she loved him and how she hoped that at some future date he might find it in himself to forgive her for what she was about to do. Lord Holland's immediate response, scrawled on the back of this hysterical letter, gave little grounds for optimism: 'Lady Susan/ April 6/ She ruin'd herself, Easter day/ the 7th 1764'. This sentiment was echoed by his elder brother. In a letter to Lady Sarah, Lord Ilchester urged her to break off all relations with 'that base & treacherous wretch my ungratefull daughter' who 'contrary to her word & promises deliberately ruin'd herself, disgraced her family, acted a cruel part towards her sisters & broke her fathers & mothers heart, by matching herself with a scoundrel of so vile a profession that there are no possible means left to retrieve her; she must now pass the remainder of her unhappy life within the precincts of Drury Lane & with the company she finds there.'

The reaction of the two brothers can hardly have surprised Susan, though it is ironic that they themselves had both made clandestine marriages. Stephen Fox went through a secret wedding ceremony with his 13-year-old bride Elizabeth not just once, but twice, in order to deceive her father Thomas Horner (of the family that gave us the nursery rhyme, 'Little Jack Horner…') about her mother Susanna Strangways Horner's involvement in it. Susanna and her erstwhile lover — none other than the yet-to-be-wed Henry Fox — had plotted to marry the child off to Stephen at such a tender age in order to deter fortune-hunters.[3] And Henry Fox's wedding with Lady Caroline Lennox was such a closely-guarded secret that even the officiating clergyman was kept in the dark over the identity of the couple he was marrying. But however unorthodox the mode of the brothers' marriages, they had enhanced, rather than undermined, their status. Susan was well aware that in her case the reverse was true.

Indeed, she had anticipated ostracism in her letter to Lord Holland. She realised the enormity of what she was doing and while the love affair was still secret had succumbed to a bout of illness, causing Henry Fox to comment in a letter to his brother: 'Lady Suke is so strong & hardy that I am surpris'd she should be indispos'd.' And though inclined to fat, she had grown so thin that

---

[3] Although Elizabeth's wedding dress, preserved at Melbury, is shockingly a child's garment, there is no suggestion of paedophilia in this match; the newly-weds were not permitted to cohabit until Elizabeth had reached the age of 16.

after the marriage her aunt Charlotte Digby (the only sister of Lord Ilchester and Lord Holland) remarked on the great strain she appeared to be labouring under.[4]

Yet so pronounced was her pride — and her belief in the rightness of her choice of partner — that she refused to knuckle under in the way, for example, Lady Sarah would do a few years later when she aroused similar ire in the family for having a child by a lover and then leaving her husband. In the wrong as she clearly was, Sarah did the 'right' thing in renouncing the world and lying low for some years. Susan was not prepared to wear sackcloth and ashes and repent of her sin in marrying the man she loved even if that might have gone some way towards mollifying her outraged family. Instead, she fought tooth and nail to win them round to her point of view.

Lady Sarah now found herself being appealed to by all parties. She had to pretend she had known nothing of the burgeoning romance until it had become common knowledge, though in fact she had been privy to the secret from the start, egging on Susan to send O'Brien the poetic *billet doux* – 'In my silence see the Lover,/ True Love is by silence known;/ In my eyes you'll best discover/ All the power of your own'[5] — that alerted him to the nature of Lady Susan's interest in him. But if her opinion was to carry any weight in conversations with Lord and Lady Ilchester, as well as with her brother-in-law Lord Holland, they had to believe in her innocence. To which end Susan set about convincing her aunt Charlotte Digby (the only close family member she was permitted to see in the immediate aftermath of her marriage) that she had deliberately kept Lady Sarah in the dark over what was going on. Her clinching argument was that Sarah's honesty was so well known that to have confided in her would have put an intolerable burden on her.

Susan also confessed to her aunt that she herself had been the prime mover in the affair with William O'Brien, who would not have had the temerity to woo her had she not taken the initiative. All of which information Charlotte Digby passed on to her brother Lord Holland.

While Susan's father and uncle were of one mind over her 'ruin', her

---

[4] Charlotte Fox's marriage to Edward Digby (d. 1746) initiated a series of alliances between the two Dorset landowning families of Fox-Strangways and Digby, owners of Melbury and Sherborne Castle respectively, so that they almost became a single family, as Lady Susan later wrote in her journal – not entirely approvingly.

[5] The second and last verse of Voltaire's lines addressed 'to Lady Hervey' (written, apparently in English, in 1726, or thereabouts), of which the first goes: 'Hervey, would you know the passion/ You have kindled in my breast?/ Trifling is the inclination/ That by words can be express'd…'

mother (with whom she was permitted to correspond but not to meet) and her aunt put pressure on Lord Holland to do something for the couple, if only as part of an exercise in damage limitation. Above all, if O'Brien would give up the disreputable profession of acting and the couple could be persuaded to live quietly in the country, then in a few years' time the scandal would die down and they would cease to be an embarrassment to the family. But in the interim, some recompense would have to be made to O'Brien for forfeiting his livelihood if the couple were not to starve. Given Lord Ilchester's refusal even to discuss the subject, let alone to come up with a plan, the women had no alternative but to appeal to Lord Holland, who — though his political influence was waning — still had friends at court.

For their part, Susan and O'Brien were prepared to do almost anything short of renouncing one another to offset the great wrong they had done and heal the family rift. O'Brien did not even need to be persuaded to give up his profession; he had already done so, having made his last appearance on stage on the eve of his wedding.

Theatrical works of reference and biographical dictionaries assert that William O'Brien was the 'son of a fencing master'. The phrase seems to have originated in a footnote in Genest's early nineteenth-century history of the English stage, explaining O'Brien's superior skill at drawing a sword on stage. The other common claim is that he was related to earlier O'Briens ennobled as Viscounts Clare who, in the words of the entry on him in the *Oxford Dictionary of National Biography*, 'having lost their fortunes supporting the Stuart cause, joined the Irish Brigade in France'.

The idea that he came of good stock, fallen upon hard times, is certainly one that O'Brien himself promoted. In an autobiographical sketch he wrote towards the end of his life and attached to his will, he says that his father was an officer in the Irish Brigade in the service of France and his grandfather 'was one of those Gentlemen who from their attachment to the unfortunate & infatuated monarch James 2nd & the religion of their ancestors, follow'd him after the Capitulation of Limerick into France'.

In this curious document he refers darkly to a person who, 'though under obligations to me, from motives of the lowest spleen and malice, took every means, by reports and by the Press, to calumniate & misrepresent me'. Yet his own description of his origins — involving a shipwreck off the coast of

Wales, his mother's death in childbirth in London, followed swiftly by the (unexplained) death in France of a father whom he'd never seen, causing him to fall 'into the hands of strangers' who, though namesakes, were apparently unrelated to him — reads more like the opening of a picaresque novel than an authentic record. As an Irish playwright of a later generation would famously put it, while losing one parent might be regarded as a misfortune, 'to lose both looks like carelessness'.

O'Brien's account certainly raises more questions than it answers. All he tells us about his mother is that she was 'a McCarty of the Family of Spring House, in the county of Tipperary'; and the sparse details he provides of his father and grandfather are based entirely on hearsay. There is no mention of a fencing master. If it was his father who taught him swordsmanship, it can only have been his adoptive father since by his own account he had never met his biological father. Bizarrely, he gives no details whatsoever about his adoptive family, the 'strangers' who — he asks us to believe — took him in solely on the grounds of a shared (and not uncommon) Irish surname. He devotes several sentences to a man — possibly a 'Catholic Priest' – who taught him French and Latin and the rudiments of Greek, recalling that he was 'a good man, but with so many singularities & oddities, that I was oftener & more seriously employ'd in playing him tricks than in profiting by his instructions'. Yet he has nothing to say of the couple who brought him up.

O'Brien seems to be aware of the sketchiness of his account, or at least that it needs some underpinning. Admitting uncertainty over his age – 'I may be more, but I cannot be less than seventy' – he attributes his vagueness to 'having lately been attack'd so severely in my head'. Is this responsible for the selectivity of his memory, or is there a simpler explanation? Could it be that the O'Briens who were not related to the Viscounts Clare were his actual parents and the farrago of namesakes and supposed antecedents is a romantic fantasy dreamed up by someone who, having married above his station, wants to lay claim to a similar status?

But whatever his origins, O'Brien made a good impression on people he met. He had excellent manners and could hold his own in the best society; he was a boon companion, lively and intelligent, as well as gentle and considerate; he made friends easily and was loyal to the friends he made. However bitterly Lady Susan's family deplored the match, they received nothing but favourable reports of O'Brien's behaviour. Mrs Digby told Lord Holland that her son Willy had 'taken a good deal of pain to enquire into the private character of the man & is assur'd from some he can depend upon that he is remarkably good natur'd & generous, has a great deal of Vanity but a good heart & not much debauch'd'. It is hard to find anyone who had a bad word to say about O'Brien, though the young James Boswell, proud to be breakfasting with Garrick on Friday 13 May 1763, is rather dismissive of him: 'Obrien [*sic*] the Player was there, a lively little fellow; but priggish.'

Lord Holland reluctantly yielded to the importunities of his sister and sister-in-law. He agreed to pay O'Brien an annuity of £400 (a significant sum in those days) in compensation for his loss of earnings on the stage until he could find — or be found — an alternative livelihood. To achieve this aim he involved his friend Clotworthy – 'Tatty' – Upton (later raised to the Irish peerage as Lord Templeton) and his 'man of business' with the wonderfully Dickensian name of Samuel Touchet. The best way of handling the situation, Lord Holland had decided, was to have the couple go and live abroad for some years until the scandal of their marriage was forgotten and Susan's three younger sisters were safely and suitably wedded. After that they might be permitted to return, provided they agreed to live quietly in the country.

Lord (Robert) Clive was approached over possible employment for O'Brien in India; but Clive's departure thither at that very moment and the couple' growing aversion to the project put an end to any notion of the actor O'Brien transforming himself into a nabob. The West Indies were also proposed, but never seriously considered. Someone, probably Upton (since he remained enthusiastically committed to the scheme), came up with the idea of persuading the King to grant them 20,000-acre plots of land – 'them' being Lord Ilchester, Lord Holland and Tatty Upton himself — in North America, which the O'Briens would develop and thereby make a fortune. Touchet proposed a sure-fire way of doing this, which was by growing a particular kind of flax to be used in the making of fine cambrics, and he took O'Brien to a plantation in Winchelsea in which he had an interest to learn the rudiments of its cultivation. A willing but bewildered O'Brien played his part, earnestly taking notes on the finer points of flax-growing.

But though he and Susan were ready to go to America to appease her family, they had little or no idea of what to expect there; all they could do was listen to their advisors who, as it turned out, were mostly as ignorant as they were. The one exception, whose name was Adam Drummond, was dismissive of the notion of cultivating flax as a means of making a fortune; he told Lord Holland that though he did not wish to dampen Touchet's ardour, 'a scheme of this kind can never in any way answer near to these sanguine expectations'. But when Drummond met the O'Briens, he was careful not to disillusion them so close to the time of their departure for America. He was impressed by O'Brien's enthusiasm and only hoped the inevitable 'small disappointments' would not discourage him. As he reported to Lord Holland: 'I thought in his manner and whole behaviour that Night He show'd a Great Disposition to Good Nature, but rather something of Levity and Giddyness which might arise from His Hurry of thought att such a time…'

Alas, poor William, earnestly contemplating the manufacture of flax on the banks of the Mohawk River when he might have been strutting the boards at Drury Lane to the grateful applause of an adoring society audience. No wonder he was prone to attacks of levity and giddiness. Drummond was not the only person to notice that, despite her upbringing, Lady Susan was blessed with a more practical turn of mind than her thespian husband. The success of their American venture was going to depend at least as much on her as it would on him.

At the beginning of September 1764 she wrote rather pathetically to her uncle, 'I can't leave England my dear Lord Holland without thanking you again & ten thousand times over for sending me, for indeed I see all the necessity for my going, and am as thankful as possible for it.' She pleaded with him for generous treatment of her old governess 'poor Mrs Trengrouse' who had, wittingly or otherwise, acted as go-between for her and O'Brien, carrying their letters to and fro. (Her plea fell on deaf ears; Lord Holland replied that he would cheerfully see Mrs T 'hang'd at Tyburn'.)

The O'Briens travelled from London to Falmouth, whence the packet (mail ship) in which they had the 'best accommodation' – thanks to Mr Touchet — left for New York on 17 September. The long coach journey through familiar West Country scenes to Falmouth was a severe test of Susan's resolve. Touchet reported that though she had been 'in good health & spirits' when he had parted with her at Stockbridge, he had subsequently heard from O'Brien that 'she seem'd much cast down in passing through Dorset without seeing one friend or relation'. Susan was deeply hurt that no one from her family had come to wave her goodbye and wish her Godspeed as she went into indefinite exile at their behest.

All things considered, it is hard to imagine a couple as ill-equipped for a pioneering life in the wilds of colonial America as the highborn Lady Susan and her Irish actor husband.

2
MERCHANTS AND MOHAWKS

The O'Briens landed in New York at the end of October. It had been a remarkably speedy Atlantic crossing for the time of year, taking only thirty-four days. But, as O'Brien wrote to David Garrick's brother George, 'between you and I, the tempest we have been used to see on dry land, before a crowded house, is far pleasanter than some we met with on the American coast…' He admitted to saying his 'short prayers' and added: 'Lady Susan was vastly ill the whole way.'

She may have been seasick, as well as homesick; but there is another possibility. Only weeks before her departure, Tatty Upton had written to Lord Holland: 'Lady Susan I think pretty advanced with child. I bantered Her about it & she did not deny it.' A little later, when arrangements for the voyage to America were already far advanced, Touchet reported that she was 'very sick at my house one morning ye week before last when I ask'd Mr Obrien if she was breeding & he said she was'.

But Lady Ilchester didn't believe it; she told Lord Holland that from what Mrs Trengrouse, who had stayed for a week with Susan, had told her, 'I should rather think there is nothing in what you hear of her being Breeding'. Had she thought that Susan might be pregnant, her mother would surely have worried about consigning her to what Adam Drummond called 'a long and Disagreeable Voyage att the most Dangerous season of the year' – though any qualms Lady Ilchester may have had on that score were brushed aside by her brother-in-law, who painted a rosy picture of what Susan's life in America would be like and a correspondingly grim one of what her remaining in London, mixing with the likes of the actor Samuel Foote '& all ye lowest of people', would mean. 'Your letters,' she gratefully replied to Lord Holland, 'are so comfortable about Susans situation abroad & so expressive about what it is & may be at Home that I assure you I would not but have her go on any account…'

If Susan was indeed pregnant, then she must have miscarried on the voyage out since there is no further mention of her 'breeding'.

New York was not then a big city, though it was the seat of civil and military government – 'the place to which all the money for the Exigencies of America is sent from Britain'. It had a population of about 20,000 and fewer than 3,000 houses. Lord Adam Gordon, MP for Aberdeenshire, who made a fact-finding tour of North America at this time, compared it unfavourably with Philadelphia 'in Beauty, regularity, Size'. The O'Briens were likewise unimpressed. William told George Garrick that it was a primitive place: 'Every thing appears just in the bud, a world in its infancy; which to folks used to the conveniences and luxuries of London appear[s] at first sight rather awkward.' Susan was more forthright, describing it to Lord Holland as 'barren & uncultivated' and writing to Lady Sarah, 'the town is not half so good as the very *worst* part of Bury[-St-Edmunds].'

The O'Briens discovered on their arrival that their story had gone before them. The tight-knit community of army officers from Fort George and wealthy settlers of British extraction knew all about the earl's daughter who had run away with Garrick's protégé, the promising Irish actor. The social elite of DeLanceys, Watts', Coldens, 'Lord' Stirling and Col. James Robertson, most of whom Adam Drummond had informed of the O'Briens' impending arrival, were curious about the infamous couple — but also apprehensive.

The leading merchant John Watts wrote to a friend in London that Lady Susan might 'be assur'd of every friendly office out of tenderness to her situation & respect to her family. But the outrageous precident to a Mans family of Girls just rising into Life, is a Burlesque on all Duty, obedience or delicacy. The more noble the worse'. And Oliver DeLancey told Drummond he would 'do them all the service in my power though I am a little fearfull of an Example to three Girls that may govern their conduct by seeing the Respect I shew to those that have Disobliged their Parents'. DeLancey admitted that his own marriage had been of much the same sort, but said that he hoped that was now forgotten and 'the Girls may not take Husbands at their own Hands'.

Despite setting such a bad example, the O'Briens made a good impression on these prominent New Yorkers. Lord Stirling (as William Alexander, though unsuccessful in his claim to that earldom, continued to call himself) made the thirty-mile journey from Basking Ridge in New Jersey to New York to pay his respects and 'found them in the hurry of receiving the Civillities of all the principal people of the place, whose best wishes to them are already engaged by the amiable ease of Lady Susan and the propriety of Mr O'Brien's behaviour'.

But Susan was struggling to come to terms with the reality of her situation in New York. Her lodgings there would have borne a closer resemblance to O'Brien's rented villa in Dunstable than to such properties as Melbury or Holland House. Living in cramped conditions was only a part of what she had to endure. Having the social status of an earl's daughter but lacking the wherewithal to go with it put her — and her husband — in an awkward position in relation to New York society. To John Watts, Susan was 'the poor unhappy Lady who I am afraid will never come right', and O'Brien 'a poor devil marrying above himself without independency, a toad under a harrow, when before he might have ap'd Caesar himself, had a merry light heart, & have got six or seven hundred a year by it, independent as a prince'.

The O'Briens' New York acquaintances were sympathetic with their plight. The phrase 'poor Lady Susan' keeps cropping up, as when Col. James Robertson, on a visit to London the following year, told Adam Drummond that 'poor Lady Susan' had 'gain'd the Hearts of all the People there'. But the colonel also noticed how volatile she was — at times 'in tolerable spirits and very entertaining, but often is in Deep Melancholy, and on little triffling Incidents… she all at once falls into a Flood of Tears' – and how O'Brien 'keeps very much at home with her and will hardly stay an Hour at the Coffee house when he is uneasy to Return because she is Alone'.

Robertson was shocked at the amount the O'Briens had spent on freight charges for the 'Useless Bulky Furniture' they had brought over with them. In money matters generally O'Brien was 'one of the most thoughtless Helpless men' he had ever known; Lady Susan, despite her upbringing, was 'a vast deal more thrifty than He', and he didn't think O'Brien 'could ever turn out well to take any great charge in any Business'. Yet he was impressed by the man's sobriety and good nature, as well as his readiness 'to suffer any Banishment to go where Lord Ilchester might desire, knowing the uneasiness He had created to that Noble Family' – though he also expressed concern to Drummond (who duly reported it to Lord Holland) that if something were not done for them, they would soon be back in England.

Uppermost in the young couple's minds was the question of the land grants on which their future in America depended. In Susan's last letter to Lord Holland before their departure from England, she had written in some bewilderment of their forthcoming voyage: 'Mr Croghan goes with us; he is a very good humour'd merry man for a companion but I don't understand that he is likely to be of any great use to us in the way of business, as he lives at Philadelphia & is a Col. in the army — however any thing that he can [do] I dare say he will.'

Susan's uncertainty over the usefulness of their travelling companion betrays her ignorance of the land situation in America and how closely intertwined it was with 'Indian Affairs'. George Croghan was principal deputy to Sir William Johnson, Sole Superintendent of the Indian Department. Both men — like O'Brien — were Irish and, having first-hand experience of colonialism at home, had an intuitive understanding of native Americans that the English lacked. This enabled them to have a foot in both the Indian camp and that of the settlers; each, for example, had Indian lovers and half-Indian children as well as European families. Though Susan was right that Croghan was based in Pennsylvania — he was responsible for the western Indians on the Ohio river — what she did not know was that he was a key figure in this tight little 'Irish fiefdom' whose head, Johnson, would be essential to the O'Briens if they were to have a future on the Mohawk river. Even before they left Falmouth, Croghan had alarmed O'Brien by informing him that without the land grant in his hand he would get nowhere in New York.

Now they sought the advice of their New York acquaintances and what they learned was not encouraging. The acting Governor, Cadwallader Colden told them the lands at Canajoharie on the Mohawk River had been 'granted long ago, & all settled above twenty miles back'. Colden also corresponded with Lord Holland, informing him that the 'purchasing of Lands of the Indians at this time… must be attended with great expence, probably more than the lands are worth'. The 'Nation' had grown greedy – 'they have of late been taught to value themselves very highly' – and, as a result, he recommended looking at the vacant land to the 'East side of the Waters between Crown Point & Ticonderoga' (Lake George). Over the next few years other sites, such as the Connecticut River, would also be suggested.

Aside from the location of their lands, there was the crucial question of what kind of return on them the O'Briens might expect. Here, too, they were in for a disappointment. Buying land in America might be a good investment for future generations, but — as Susan was quick to inform Lord Holland – 'no one attempts to lay out any thing themselves, as they have the impossibility of ever gaining the least advantage of it'. Indeed, Sir William Johnson, whose influence with the Indians made him paramount in land negotiations in the province of New York, could only attract settlers on the plots he had purchased by letting them live rent-free for several years — he did not expect to make a farthing out of his lands in either his own or his son's lifetime. Cultivating flax on the banks of the Mohawk River, which had seemed such a good idea in London, now struck Susan as 'an absolute impossibility & wou'd be madness to think of'.

As time went on Susan would become increasingly exasperated by her friends' refusal to take her word on the land situation and at one point begged Tatty Upton to come and see for himself – 'for my accounts I see plainly are not believ'd, though I am not such a foolish nonsensical girl as to write a parcel of lies because I don't like this country'.

Meanwhile there was a storm brewing at home that threatened to crush Susan completely.

The first warning came from Samuel Touchet, who wrote: 'my Lord Holland is so angry with your Ladyship in laying out so much in cloaths for yourself & Mr Obrien, wch he says ought to have been reserv'd for the improvement of your lands, that he'll not write…'

The enormity of the O'Briens' expenditure in equipping themselves for their new life had only just been made known to Lord Holland. Touchet had been understandably reluctant to break the news of O'Brien's debts to his tailor and others of over £500 and of the couple's spending spree during their last fortnight in London – 'I thought we shd never have done with new wants, and tradesmens bills hourly coming in that I knew nothing of'. But he could not wish away a total of over £2,000 (more than double the estimated amount and a huge figure in those days) that Lord Ilchester would have to pay, even though Touchet offered to pay £500 out of his own pocket rather than 'add one minute's uneasiness to ye distress he must feel in having so well accomplish'd a daughter throw herself so foolishly away'. It would not have been the first time, he said, that he had suffered for his good nature.

Lady Sarah also alerted Susan to Lord Holland's fury over the accounts — for making 'your father pay for swords, guns &c for Mr O'Brien', not to mention his portrait, which he 'cannot forgive'. Susan noted in the margin of this letter that O'Brien's portrait had in fact been 'painted and paid for two or three years before' and the bill from the artist Francis Cotes was for *her* portrait. But in an age when letters took more than a month to cross the Atlantic, such misunderstandings could fester in the minds of the offended parties. In this instance, Touchet had been able to correct the error and also explain to Lord Holland that the 'fire arms' had been bought on Mr Croghan's advice as necessary equipment for the Mohawk country, where they were supposedly headed. But he could not explain away the total of £2080.14.5d, which included a coach for Lady Susan and many other items her family regarded as frivolous in her 'reduced circumstances'.

Lord Ilchester's reaction was more resigned than angry; he told his brother 'you are much too good to be at half the trouble and expence you are on account of my worthless daughter'. Yet 'bad as she is,' he confessed, 'it is impossible for me not to feel for her but I will struggle & try to forget her totally, as not the least palliating excuse can be made for her…'

Lord Holland would not contact Susan directly but had Touchet write at his dictation that 'he saw no prospect of any thing but your ruin, that… you seem'd to be bent on setting out in so extravagant & expensive a way of life that it was in vain for him to think of serving you, that he expects to hear Mr Obrien is in jail at New York before ye year comes round, and that it might well have been so here before his debts had been paid.' Touchet concluded the letter by saying that Lord Holland had forbidden him to pay anything more on his or Lord Ilchester's account except the £400 in quarterly payments for the foreseeable future.

The effect on Susan of this verbal onslaught, at one remove, from the man on whom she was dependent for a living was devastating. Lady Ilchester, in one of her letters, added fuel to the fire by calling her 'an abandon'd castaway'. New York friends had already noticed her emotional brittleness and volatility, how her mood would swing wildly from hope to despair, from melancholy to euphoria and back again. In the depths of winter, far from a home that was no longer welcoming, and threatened with destitution, Susan might have broken down completely but for the support of a husband whose devotion was exemplary.

She did not deny that she had wronged her parents. She deeply regretted the purchases she and O'Brien had made before leaving England, but argued in her reply to Lord Holland that they only bought things they had been told were necessary for them to have, and 'after all indeed my Lord our intelligence had been mostly false in ev'ry thing'. Furthermore, it was all done in such a hurry they had no time to reflect and little idea of how much they'd spent. She ended her letter with a plea to her uncle to 'have compassion on Her you once lov'd so much' and to continue to protect her — for 'what shall I do, what will become of me if you don't?'

Lord Holland did eventually write her a letter, which was several pages long and far from reassuring. 'Dear Madam,' he began — not 'Minx' or 'Lady Suke' or any of his former terms of endearment. He conceded that his message had been 'such as must vex you'. While he'd been under the misapprehension that the family was being asked to pay for O'Brien's portrait, he had been more angry than ever before in his life; but that had been an error, which Touchet had discovered, and 'your buying your own Picture was only a Levity, and of a piece with the rest of your Bills'. What these demonstrated was that 'you had never thought of what your situation was'.

That was the nub of the matter, her refusal to recognise and conform to her 'unhappy fate'. The fact that he could see no remedy did not mean he did not care. His brother had always said, 'She has ruin'd herself and all attempts to help her are in vain. You are trying to bring one absolutely dead to Life again. I will do what you advise me because I have no scheme of my own. But I declare I have not the least hope in any.' Lord Holland shared his brother's view (but not 'without the utmost concern') and said that 'nothing would have been propos'd but for Ly Ilchester's Tears & Grief & inordinate Desire that Mr Obryen should leave the Stage'. Everything that had been done was due to her; Lord Holland had merely been carrying out her wishes.

He denied that he had been responsible for her going to America, telling her that he had instructed both Upton and Touchet to ensure that she did not go 'unless it was your own Opinion that it was the best thing for you'. Had she chosen to stay put, Lord Holland went on, he would have been obliged to 'have continually been painting to you your miserable situation here' and that 'would have been cruel', besides being useless. It was impossible that he should regard her marriage in the same light as she did. 'No Madam,' he went on, warming to his theme and addressing Susan as if she were a political adversary he was intent on browbeating, 'when Mr O'Brien and you met you were both undone.'

Her reference to the warmth of his earlier letters failed to move him, since that intimacy had not induced her to confide in him in return – 'I was the Person from whom the secret was most strictly kept'. If she had taken him into her confidence, 'it had been proper to have shew'd you the Misery of your Union.' He believed he might then have been able to prevent it: 'But no more of this...'

Yet he had plenty more to say. If he and Mr Upton had been deceived about the lands (he had been the less deceived, but Upton's greater credulity was entirely due to his 'Friendship & Goodness'), then that merely confirmed what he had thought from the beginning, namely that the situation was 'without a Remedy'.

Nor should she expect great things in the way of a place for Mr O'Brien. Ministers would say to him, '*Shall we reward Mr O'Brien for marrying your Niece? Who will carry his name to the King?*' The King himself had told the politician Wellbore Ellis that 'he hop'd to God Lord Holland did not mean to ask the smallest Rank *from Him* for Mr O'Brien; though sorry to refuse me, nothing should prevail with Him to grant it.' Even the land grants, however worthless they turned out to be, had not passed without some murmuring: 'Mr O'Brien's name blasts everything.'

Lord Holland did not blame him for being an Irishman of Roman Catholic stock (and therefore barred from holding civil or military office in England by the Test and Corporation Acts of 1673) and was prepared to concede that O'Brien had not 'done any wrong since that very great wrong that ruin'd himself & you'. But how could Susan imagine they could ever have got a place in England, or lived there on a footing 'tolerable to yourself or Friends'?

If O'Brien had got so heavily into debt as a single man, how was he going to live within his income as a married one? What Lord Holland resented most was his saying that he couldn't live in New York on the £400 a year he was providing. But when all was said and done, 'it was not the Money so much as your apparent view in the Expence that vex'd me'.

Despite the bleakness of Lord Holland's message — with its stress on O'Brien's unacceptability and the impossibility of her own social rehabilitation — Susan clung to his statement that he was not going to abandon them to their fate: 'as you say despair shall not prevent your kind endeavours,' she wrote in reply, 'so I cannot allow it to prevent my hopes in the success of them.'

It was fortunate that Lord Holland's letter had arrived when she was in a buoyant mood, hopeful of obtaining for O'Brien the Secretaryship of the Province of New York. That, she told her uncle, would more than fulfil their hopes and expectations, and would make them 'very happy for the rest of their lives'. The current holder of the post, a Mr Clarke, lived in England and employed a deputy to carry out the work; and it's likely that Susan hoped to be able to do the same in due course, though she wisely refrained from mentioning that to Lord Holland.

Like the business of the lands, the negotiations over the Secretaryship of New York dragged on and on. But even Touchet, whose partiality for Lady Susan tended to make him enthuse over any opportunity, was from the outset less than sanguine about this one. He told her, 'I don't find Mr Clarke shews any disposition to part with the patent, nor do we think it could be got in Mr O'Brien's name if Mr Clarke would resign.'

The O'Briens made their first excursion outside New York in June 1765. They went to visit Sir William Johnson at his settlement on the Mohawk River. They wanted to see what land might be theirs and get Sir William's views of the practicality of the scheme at first hand.

They travelled by boat as far as Albany and, as Susan noted on a later journey up the Hudson, 'Nothing can be more delightful than the navigation of this beautifull River, for 150 miles up it, its banks afford an agreeable variety of cultivated & savage beauties, & its stream is never interrupted by the shallows & rapids which are generally met with in the Rivers with which North America abounds.' Susan was less impressed with Albany – 'the 2nd town of so large a province as NY,' she noted, 'is but a very poor one.' She called its inhabitants 'altogether Dutch, & so attach'd to their old customs & manners that much less improvement has been made here than in most other places considering that it was settled so long ago'.

The Scottish traveller, Lord Adam Gordon, who was also visiting Sir William Johnson, called Albany 'dull and ill built' with 'very dirty and crooked' streets. He was as critical as Susan of its Dutch inhabitants, who displayed 'an unwearied attention to their own personal and particular Interests, and an abhorrence of all superiour powers'.

The notorious Stamp Act, a new tax on all paper — not just legal documents and licenses, but newspapers and other publications, even playing cards — had been passed in the English parliament in March that year. Supposedly a measure to raise money to pay for British troops garrisoned in North America, it was in reality part of the Prime Minister George Grenville's attempt to recoup the enormous expenses of the Seven Years' War with France. It was deeply unpopular with the colonists, whose cry was 'No taxation without representation'. Riots became commonplace, and Gordon learned that a number of troops had been sent to Albany 'to prevent the entire and total Destruction of all the buildings and Stores belonging to the King, which was but too well effected before their arrival'. Having no loyalty to king and country, the descendants of the original Dutch settlers were even more disaffected than their fellow colonists of British descent.

The O'Briens didn't linger in Albany but pursued their journey up the

Mohawk River to Fort Johnson. Sir William's new settlement was about fourteen miles overland from there. Lord Adam Gordon noted that the Superintendent of Indian Affairs for the Northern District had built himself a very comfortable house he named Johnson Hall in a clearing in the forest. The soil there was excellent, producing all sorts of grain with no need of manure, and the place was usually crowded with Mohawks. Though Gordon was impressed by Sir William and paid him a second visit some months later, he shuddered at the thought of living in such close proximity to the Indian braves and squaws: 'no consideration should tempt me to lead his life — I suppose custom may in some degree have reconciled him to it, but I know no other man equal to so disagreeable a duty.'

On 20 June, Johnson wrote to the acting Governor of New York, Cadwallader Colden: 'I have had Lord Adam Gordon & Ly Susan O'Brien & Her Husband here, the Two latter spoke to me a good deal, on the Subject of their Land...' Knowing that the location of the O'Brien land was still unsettled, Sir William proposed that, all else failing, he procure an additional tract adjacent to his own at Canajoharie, which he would divide with him, provided the king approved of the grant. He made it clear that no one else had sufficient clout with the Indians to make such a deal.

How the O'Briens spent their time at Johnson Hall, when they weren't discussing land, must be a matter of conjecture. An early biographer of Sir William paints an idyllic picture of Susan, 'the scion of a noble house', and her host's 'housekeeper' Molly Brand (actually his Indian mistress and mother of several of his children), going on 'many a ramble... in the greenwood' together, citing letters of Lady Susan's in which she refers to her companion as 'a well-bred and pleasant lady'. These letters, if they ever existed, seem to have vanished. As does the one in which the biographer claims that Sir William begged Lord Holland 'that the young couple might again be received into the good grace of his family — urging amongst other things, that O'Brien seemed to be a very worthy young man, possessing, in the highest degree, the affections of his wife'.

Johnson may well have warmed to his Irish compatriot and his wife — and they to him. But it's unlikely that the prospect of 'housekeeping among the Mohawks', as the witty New Yorker John Watts put it, appealed to either of the O'Briens. Sir William's early biographer's Rousseauistic account of the noblewoman and the noble savage is affecting, but Susan's reaction to their host's lifestyle was probably more in keeping with Lord Adam Gordon's.

On their return to New York the O'Briens spent the remaining summer months at country estates on Long Island and in New Jersey while their friends in London laboured on their behalf. Despite Lord Holland's admission of his and Mr Upton's 'error… about Land', over which 'Mr Drummond undeceiv'd me very early', Upton continued to promote the scheme enthusiastically. He advised Susan to consult the newly-appointed Governor of New York, Sir Henry Moore, and the military commander-in-chief of North America, General Thomas Gage.[6] Susan's irritation is evident in a comment pencilled in the margin of his letter: 'Gen. Gage & every body at NY laugh'd at the whole scheme.'

The arrival of the families of both the incoming Governor of New York and the army officer Major R.F. Cary, who had been a beneficiary of Lord Holland's influence over promotion (and hoped for further advancement), enlarged the O'Briens' social circle — and Mrs Cary, in particular, provided William with a suitable subject for satire. Like many of his classically educated contemporaries who would not have described themselves as poets, O'Brien was much given to versification, generally in light-hearted imitation of Pope, to amuse himself and his friends.

In 'A Newfoundlander to Mrs Cary', he adopts a Canadian persona in order to pay elaborate tribute to his muse:

> Oh had you seen what I saw late last night,
> An Earthly Goddess cloath'd in heavenly white,
> Her bosom as a new born infant — bare!
> Mute as a mackerel at her did I stare
> Admiring now her skin & now her Hair;…
> …What tho' the grave matrons call you wild,
> And say that you neglect your dear sweet child,
> Regardless dress, nor mind their envious prate,
> Dress & appear the Queen of Love in state!
> But there's the rub, these ladies can't abide
> To see you shew those beauties they all hide,
> Or rather wish they had to hide; for then

---

[6] General Thomas Gage was the second son of the first Viscount Gage and was an experienced army officer and colonial administrator. According to the *ODNB*, a 'harsh but fair epitaph might have been "Good soldier but no warrior"'.

No doubt like you they'd gladly treat ye men.
Go on great woman! mind not what they say
But shew a little, little more each day,
Till soon like Pitt that Patriot so famed,
You naked stand, & like him not asham'd!

Mrs Cary may have invited such treatment by boasting of her intimacy with Lady Sarah, who was 'vastly diverted' to hear of her *friendship* with Mrs Cary: 'you know she dined one day at the Pay Office. I saw her at Ranelagh [Gardens] one night this year, & went up to make her a civil speech: & that is our friendship.' Sarah was also entertained by Susan's descriptions of Mrs Cary's dress and coiffure, remarking, ''tis almost impossible to make the ladies understand that heads bigger than one's body are ugly.'

In spite of her frequent exhortations to Susan not to go out in society but to live simply, Sarah was all for her putting the likes of Mrs Cary in their place and sent her 'a pink & green lutestring ready made with all proper *accompaniments*' as a means of doing just that.

She also kept the O'Briens abreast of all that was going on in London. 'The new play of the "Clandestine Marriage" is a charming acting play,' she wrote in March 1766. She didn't know how it would read and admitted that the epilogue, though written by Garrick, was 'sad stuff'. But it was an improvement on most of the plays that were now being put on. Generally, the actors seemed to 'scream at one another like screech owls, & hollow their parts without any sense or feeling'. In a delicately turned compliment to O'Brien, she referred to 'a devil of a man called Dodd, that dares to act parts that once were so sweetly perform'd'.[7]

A couple of months later Garrick himself wrote a lengthy letter, thanking O'Brien for some garden seeds he'd sent him. He carried on in botanical vein, hoping that O'Brien would 'bring over some sweet plants of your own raising', for 'I have set my heart upon seeing a little blew-ey'd Susan, & a black-ey'd William, & I must not be disappointed' without pausing to consider whether this might not be a sensitive subject for the young and so far childless couple.

But the letter contains plentiful evidence of Garrick's more pleasing qualities: his affection for O'Brien, which shines through his patronising prose, and his eagerness to set up a fund for those actors who were too old and sick to look after themselves. It is full of theatrical gossip — who has died, whose star is waxing and whose waning, the amputation of Foote's leg after a fall

---

[7] 'Mr Dodd, of the Bath company, is engaged at Drury-lane house for next winter… to appear in Mr Obrien's cast of parts' (*London Evening Post*, 14 April 1765).

from a horse (in a foolish wager with the Duke of York) and his determination to act on one leg now that he had a patent for his theatre in the Haymarket — a new rival to both Drury Lane and Covent Garden. Garrick also mentions *The Clandestine Marriage* that he co-wrote with George Colman, which some have suggested might have been prompted by the O'Briens' marriage, though the play contains few echoes of their situation and even Garrick might have hesitated to bring up the subject if he thought it would give offence.

The effect on O'Brien of these graphic reminders of the life and promising career he had renounced for the love of Susan may easily be imagined. Soon after his arrival in New York he had begged George Garrick for news of 'Old Drury', saying how often he longed to 'take a peep thro' the Curtain, & have a frisk in the Green room'. Now George's more famous brother writes, 'I have scolded *George* for not writing to you, he is very sorry & asham'd — he serves me in the same manner & like condemn'd strumpets, pleads his belly which as it now stands, is a most apparent object of your pity & the best excuse for his Laziness.'

O'Brien's situation was frustrating. As an appendage of his wife, dependent on her family for an income, he could do nothing but wait and hope for a 'place' – now that the land grant seemed so unlikely to prove remunerative, even if the lands ever materialised. Had he been of a more energetic disposition, he might have forged an opportunity for himself. But like the future Mr Micawber he lived in almost daily expectation of something turning up.

※

At the end of 1765 Lord Holland did come up with a place for O'Brien, through the good offices of the Marquis of Granby. But 'Barrack Master at Quebec' was hardly the sort of post to set the pulse racing. Fortunately, his attendance would not be required, since there was a deputy in place to do the actual work. However, the salary was small — and the deputy must get his share. But as the estimable Mr Touchet pointed out, 'it's a beginning and I hope it will soon be followed by something more'.

The 'something more' that Susan had set her heart on was the Secretaryship of the Province of New York. Negotiations over that had stalled while Mr Clarke waited for his brother, who was visiting New York from the West Indies, to report on the situation there. But the possibility of getting this post was the only thing that kept the O'Briens on the far side of the Atlantic.

It must have been this prospect, too, that lay behind Susan's latest idea, which was to build a house in New York. Such a plan, though it would involve expense, was well received at home, where it was taken as evidence of an intention to stay put. On 8 May 1766 Lady Sarah reported from Holland House that Lord Holland was seeing Lady Ilchester that morning to discuss it, 'but I must have the pleasure to inform you that I believe you will be perfectly satisfied… for I understand she approves of it & I know Lord H has made no objection to it'. Lady Ilchester expressed a willingness to contribute 'some part' of the cost of building, since 'all your friends seem to think your settling yourself in as comfortable a way as you can in America at least for some years the most eligible scheme'.

But before anything could be resolved on that score the O'Briens had set out for Quebec so that the Barrack Master might make himself known to his deputy and acquaint himself with the situation there. They went via Niagara Falls and Montreal. The thought of their making such a journey through the wilderness excited Lady Sarah but appalled Lady Ilchester, who was glad she didn't hear of it till it was half over. Lord Adam Gordon had visited Niagara Falls several times the year before, and each time 'with more Astonishment and Satisfaction'. He doubted 'if in any part of the known World, there is any thing of the kind, so Magnificently Stupendous'.

Sarah wrote to Susan, 'I know you delighted in the thoughts of doing what no other woman ever did or will do.' And evidence of Susan's intrepidity on this trip comes from a Lieutenant Benjamin Roberts, who was the O'Briens' guide for a part of it: in a letter to Sir William Johnson, he expresses his admiration for the way she 'bore all the fatigues and bad riding with good humor and Spirit'. Much later, Lady Sarah met a 'gentlemen that went with you to Quebec'. If this was Lt. Roberts, he gave her a 'very exact and comfortable account' of Susan's appearance: 'I hear you're very fat, but look very well. I'm sure your pretty little sly face is not alter'd; what would I give to see it.'

The O'Briens' arrival in Quebec coincided with the departure of the Scottish governor of the province, James Murray, whose recall to answer charges of misconduct did not inhibit his entertainment of the couple on board the ship that was to take him back to England. In the surviving correspondence there is no indication of whether O'Brien inspected the barracks of which he was nominally master, though he and Susan would eventually return to Quebec.

Letters from home at this period are full of references to 'your American insurrections' and 'your riotous Americans' (Touchet), 'these rebellions at New York' and 'your nasty American business' (Lady Sarah), and 'your commotions' (Garrick). Garrick's attitudinising might be over the top, but his view was a common English one:

> I hope the Mother Country will not find disobedient Children among you for her great affection & lenity — If the Americans should, like some tempers (which I will not believe) grow insolent & ungratefull from her kind usage — I should cry out with Lear in the extremity of rage & sorrow – ——————— O may they feel
>
> How sharper than a serpent's tooth it is,
> To have a thankless Child!

Though Sarah worried over her beloved Susan's safety in distant America during the riots, her immediate concern was that this 'nasty American business' was keeping her husband in London. (Touchet, too, complained over the time the parliamentary debates over the Stamp Act took up.)

Letters from Sarah and from Susan's mother also voiced worries over both Lord Ilchester's and Lord Holland's health. Lord Ilchester had had a violent fever and for a fortnight was so ill that Lady Ilchester almost despaired of him; even when the fever wore off, his pulse was intermittent – 'just like a dying person but I bless God that was not the case'. Lord Holland's decline was more serious and enduring. Sarah first mentioned it in February 1766 and three months later she was writing, 'I cannot give you any satisfactory account of him, he is rather better because he eats meat now, but he does not gain at all; they begin to think there is some inward decay, tho' there is no appearance of it.' She told Susan confidentially of 'the very great alteration there is since you saw him in his temper & looks; he is so low that you can seldom get him to speak, & so touchy & peevish that the least contradiction hurts him from exerting him so much'.

The only thing that cheered him was the betrothal of his eldest son Stephen (always known as Ste) to Lady Mary Fitzpatrick, a good match despite the undesirability of an alliance with the family of the Duke of Bedford, with whom he had quarrelled politically and personally. Too ill to write to Susan himself, he dictated a letter in which he said that Ste's marriage was 'entirely of his own doing, and I believe, he has chose well, for she seems to me, very good humour'd, & perfectly well bred'. Sarah was equally enthusiastic about Lady Mary, telling her 'dear Netty' (as she had taken to calling Susan, adopting O'Brien's nickname for her), ''tis a little blessed angel, & you will love her I know, for one of my greatest pleasures in the thought of this match is that I know my dearest Netty gains a friend by her in this family, who I know will never miss an opportunity of doing a good-natured thing.'

※

After the excitement of their journey upcountry, the O'Briens found life in New York very flat on their return at the end of July 1766. There was no more talk of their building a house there. None of their schemes had made any progress and no doubt there were a number of outstanding bills they hadn't the means to pay. Sarah wrote in October that she was 'vastly sorry to find you so much out of spirits'. She apologised for not having thought of trying to get a place for O'Brien while her brother, the Duke of Richmond, was briefly (between April and July) Secretary of State, though she doubted she would have been successful. But she chided her friend for putting all the blame for the failure of her schemes on 'poor Mr Upton'.

Susan did not doubt Upton's good intentions; what aggravated her was his refusal to take any notice of what she had told him time and again. Lord Holland was at least prepared to concede that the land grant might not answer their case, but the overly sanguine Upton simply brushed aside her objections and considered himself to be better informed on what was going on in America than either of the O'Briens.

Sarah knew how unwelcome her sermonising was and later told Susan she had resolved never to offer her any more advice. Yet she could hardly refuse when a worried Lady Ilchester, hearing rumours that the O'Briens were contemplating a return to England, begged her to use her influence to prevent that. But 'after this, my dear Netty, I will never plague you again'. In an attempt to bolster Susan's spirits Sarah urged her to count her blessings – 'a perfect, happy, contented life till 20'; marriage to the man of her choice; an adequate income that her friends were intent on increasing; and, most important of all, the luck of finding that the man she loved had turned out to be worthy of her love, 'sensible, good-tempered, amiable, constant, & the best husband in the world (I have it from yourself)'.

But the words 'adequate income' merely rubbed salt in Susan's wounds. O'Brien might be the best husband in the world but he was an incorrigible spendthrift and she had to admit to Sarah — in the strictest confidence —

that they were deeply in debt and had been obliged to borrow money. All of which added to Sarah's worries on their behalf, now that Lord Holland's hold on life had become so precarious.

Nearly a year later, when Sarah wrote again, she gave Susan an account of a conversation she'd had with Lady Ilchester, who'd been indignant with her for suggesting 'you might be distressed in case of Lord Holland's death': did she imagine that Susan's mother would forsake her own daughter in her time of greatest need? Sarah had chided herself for overlooking Lady Ilchester's 'good & generous disposition', but persisted in asking her 'how she would or could serve you'.

Lady Ilchester's answer was less than reassuring. She made it plain to Sarah she would never provide Susan with income enough to enable her to be independent of *her*. Keeping her on a tight rein was the only way to ensure that she didn't act in a way she might disapprove of, though as her mother she naturally had Susan's best interests at heart.

'But, Madam,' Sarah had said, 'must she always be dependent?'

'Yes,' Lady Ilchester had replied, 'upon her mother; *that* is no great misfortune. She is not the only person in that case, & if she was, if depending on my love for her only is a mellancholly prospect (which I cannot say I think it is), she must expect some uncertainty from her situation: why did she bring it upon herself? Indeed, Lady S, I will not ask Lord I for any thing; if she will not rely wholly upon me, she is very ungrateful. If she will, she may be well contented.'

Lady Ilchester had also said that, in the event of Lord Holland's death — and Sarah didn't think she should really be telling Susan this — she would insist on Lord Ilchester's continuing to pay the £400 annuity that Lord Holland was currently paying and if he refused she would use her own money to see Susan 'well & comfortably settled'. But, Sarah added, she would not make it easy for them, 'as it entirely depended on yours & Mr O'Brien's merits towards her'.

Lord Holland himself wrote to Susan soon after this, remarking that in the all-too-likely event of his death he didn't know what would become of her. He had given up all hope of the lands in America providing her with an income and was now only interested in knowing what they might sell for, 'and what your moderate wishes are' – with the emphasis very much on 'moderate'.[8] He included some family news in his letter: Lady Holland was well; Ste had

---

[8] Lord Holland was either unable to sell his American lands or decided against doing so. In the year of his death, Susan noted that they now belonged to his third son, Colonel (later General) Henry Fox.

just left, 'carrying His most amiable wife, big with child, with Him'; Lady Sarah was 'as handsome, and flirts as much as ever'; his brother was as well as he'd ever seen him, but unalterable in his opinion that her marriage 'was ruin from the beginning'; Lady Ilchester was at Melbury and his own son Charles was in Italy.

Burdened with the huge gambling debts of both his elder sons, Ste and Charles, Lord Holland was looking for a way of stopping the annuity he was paying her. In October 1767 Lady Ilchester had written, 'Lord H proposes to give you 2000 pounds & ye annuity to cease — that ye interest of ye 2000 should produce to you a Hundred a year, tho' ye common interest would not, & that I would allow you 200# a year besides.' If that, plus the Barrack Master's salary, was not enough for them to live on in New York, then they must go to Quebec 'or some cheap place abroad, as things are circumstanc'd at present it would be madness to come home'.

There had been no response from Susan to this offer of a one-off payment in place of the annuity, as Sarah discovered when she visited Holland House in June 1768. Lord Holland would not write himself since he did 'not desire to vex Lady Susan, & finds he cannot write without offending her', but he was clearly incensed by her attitude. Once again Sarah sought to intercede. Despite her promise not to lecture, or 'plague', her 'dear Netty' more, she immediately took her to task for her lack of gratitude for all Lord Holland had done for her – '& do not say I love to show you how dependant you are, for indeed it is not ill-nature in me, but that I cannot comprehend why you should not be *proud of your obligation.*'

Sarah reminded Susan that the annuity had never been intended to continue indefinitely and that, though Lord Holland knew Susan was also getting handouts from Lady Ilchester, he hadn't reduced the amount he was paying. Then there was the Barrack Master's post, for which 'you did not even thank him' and now this – 'I have ask'd Lord H, if I could persuade you to take the £2000, whether he would still give it; he said, "Yes, if he was not dead," which I am sorry to hear him wish so often…'

Susan noted in the margin of this letter: 'No doubt much kindness has been shown *me*, & more intended. But 4 years' incessant proposals & expectations of impossibilities is enough to excuse impatience. I'm sure Mr O'B has shown less than any other man in his situation.'

The last sentence, and the emphasis on '*me*' in the first, reveal that what really riled Susan was her family's refusal to recognise O'Brien despite the good reports they'd had of his behaviour and his readiness to fall in with their plans. If she'd failed to thank Lord Holland for getting him the Barrack

Master's position, it was because she didn't consider it worthy of him (though Lord Holland was hardly to blame for that).

After this letter from Sarah there is a seven-year gap in the correspondence between the two friends. Though they continued to exchange letters, the editor of Sarah's correspondence (a twentieth-century Lord Ilchester) writes that 'Lady Susan preserved none written between June, 1768, and June, 1775'. No doubt Susan destroyed these letters out of concern for her friend's posthumous reputation.

For some time there had been signs that all was not well with Lady Sarah's marriage: in her enthusiasm for Paris, where she had gone without Charles (now, after his father's death, Sir Charles) Bunbury and had clearly turned men's heads with the flirtatious behaviour Lord Holland had mentioned as characteristic of her; in the lack of any offspring; and in the increasing amount of time the couple spent apart, Sir Charles pursuing his racing interests at Newmarket and Sarah going off whenever she could to London and Holland House, where the theatricals that had brought about Susan's downfall had been resumed. As a result, gossip was rife.

Rumours had even reached Susan in New York. As early as 23 October 1767, Sarah had thanked her dear Netty for her 'kind, sensible, & gentle way of advising me'. She was aware that 'the less a woman is talked of the better in general', but admitted she had 'the vanity to love general admiration and the folly to own it'. Yet she assured Susan her morals had not been 'spoilt by the French' and she had 'succeeded far beyond hopes' in her foremost desire, which was 'to make Sir Charles happy'.

But the stories persisted and soon enough the grounds for them became evident. Sarah embarked on a rash affair with Lord William Gordon, produced a daughter, Louisa 'Bunbury', and finally parted company with Sir Charles — to the consternation of her family. On 3 April 1769 Lady Ilchester wrote to Susan, 'I dare say Lady Sarah's sad affair is a great trouble to you. She is very infamous & Lord H dreadfully angry with her.'

Susan and Sarah were now united in adversity, as well as in friendship. But whereas Susan refused to give up the fight, the more pliable Sarah withdrew from the world to live a retired life with her daughter in a cottage on her brother's Goodwood estate.

Lord Holland's attempt to distance himself from Susan's affairs was facilitated by the more proactive part her mother was now taking. In May 1768, Touchet wrote to say that Lady Ilchester had 'obtain'd from Lord Hillsborough ye Secretaryship of ye Island of Bermuda which is not so valuable as Lord Hillsborough could wish it for Mr O'Brien, but being a Patent office for Life it was best to get it while there was a friend at Court'.

As with the Barrack Master appointment in Quebec, the duties would be performed by a deputy and the O'Briens were not obliged to move to Bermuda. Upton claimed credit for having alerted Lady Ilchester to the vacancy even before Lord Hillsborough himself knew of it. He thought it might be worth £200 or £300 a year, 'but cannot as yet learn the real value'.

Once again, hopes were raised of better things to come and six months later Touchet was confident of getting the Storekeeper's place in Quebec for O'Brien, which came with 'a good house, fire & candle' and — he'd been told — was ranked 'next to governor'.

The promise of a second place in Quebec, complete with accommodation, persuaded the O'Briens to consider moving there — a decision that delighted Lady Ilchester, who wrote, 'I dare say it will make a great difference as to the saving scheme — which I think a very right one – & as you seem so anxious to behave properly & please us I do hope & make no doubt but that we shall meet again.' But the harmony between mother and daughter was short-lived.

On 14 May 1769 Susan wrote not to her mother but to Lady Holland, informing her of O'Brien's determination to return to England in the autumn. She pointed out they had now been nearly five years in America, 'and find by experience that it is impossible for us to live within our income'. Their disillusionment was total; they had no inducement 'to remain in a country vastly expensive, vastly disagreeable', where — and here Susan was wildly overstating the case – 'we cannot make a usefull Friend or even a pleasant acquaintance'.

After five years they could no longer delude themselves with 'vain hopes' that their circumstances were going to change. Back in England, they could live quietly in the country and 'with resignation I hope allways to enjoy, wait a more favourable moment than we have hitherto experienc'd when Lord Holland's endeavours, or some unexpected good fortune, may render us a little more independent'. There, she believed, 'we could contract our expences to our income, and not be involved in difficultys which are unavoidable here'. Though Mr O'Brien could 'never repent coming' – for that was the only way he could have demonstrated his willingness to do whatever the family asked of him — he saw all too plainly 'the ruin of continuing'. The one thing that was holding them back was 'the fear of doing any thing contrary to the opinion of my Friends'.

O'Brien expressed his disenchantment privately, and in verse. 'On an American Spring' evokes the delights of spring in Britain, 'But here alas! how different the scene' – noisy frogs, bitter north winds, no bird song. Even the poor 'exil'd' cow, giving milk in town, eating old shoes and lying down on flint, seems miserable –

> Methinks I hear her thus declare her mind
> In lowings louder than the Northern wind —
> 'Cursed be the wretch that first the ocean crost
> 'And gave a name to this detested coast,
> 'Who rob'd the savages of what was meant
> 'By nature, to give savages content;
> 'And found a place of torment e'er we die
> 'For man as well as beast to freeze & fry!
> 'Ah! where is May that us'd to bring me food
> 'And send me to the meads in merry mood,
> 'In Britain's Isle she stays, ye Gods ah why,
> 'Why was I forc'd to this curs'd place to fly!...'

When Lady Ilchester learned of the O'Briens' plan to return to England, she threatened to undo the 'several good offices' she had done with Susan's father and 'not leave you a sixpence at my death, which otherwise — had you been guided by me — I intended to do'. She urged Susan to try and dissuade O'Brien from coming. 'Have patience a year longer,' she pleaded, 'yr coming just after this shocking affair of Lady Sarah's would make you still more forlorn.'

In the teeth of such opposition, the O'Briens thought better of returning straightaway. They reverted to the family-approved plan of going to Quebec and left New York in September 1769 on what had become almost a familiar journey up the Hudson River to Albany, then northwards through the wild Mohawk country, where they'd once hoped to make their fortune, into Canada.

The reality of what awaited them in Quebec was — inevitably — quite different from what Touchet had promised in his letter about the Storekeeper's place, with its high rank and good accommodation. Susan cryptically noted: 'Neither respectable — neither a house or coals &c.' They stuck it out for a year (as Lady Ilchester had asked), then — without consulting the family — set sail for England in the late summer of 1770, arriving in September.

Their precipitate action in quitting Quebec cost O'Brien the storekeeper's post. Horace Walpole's friend, General Conway, who was 'labouring to reform the ordnance department', ordered all officers to return to their posts. O'Brien refused to go and was summarily dismissed despite the interposition — as Walpole called it — of Lord and Lady Holland.

Nearly half a century later, when Susan read John Adolphus's *History of England from the Accession of George III to the Conclusion of Peace in 1783*, she reflected on the early part of the American 'contest', which she had 'in a manner' witnessed. Writing in her journal, she dismissed the Stamp Act as 'an injudicious experiment' and shook her head over 'the folly, the madness of repeated administrations'. Their smallest fault, she reckoned, was their 'total ignorance of the state, the habits, & the disposition of the Colonists'. Far worse was that they would neither be instructed nor informed. 'In national concerns,' she went on, 'the conduct was similar to what *we* experienced as individuals. *Our* friends raving of the advantages of cultivating Lands in America, no representations of *ours* would undeceive them, till length of time, & the immense expence necessary to make any settlements, brought them at last to think as they should have done long before; & they repeal'd *our Stamp Act* when it was too late for *us* to follow any other project.'

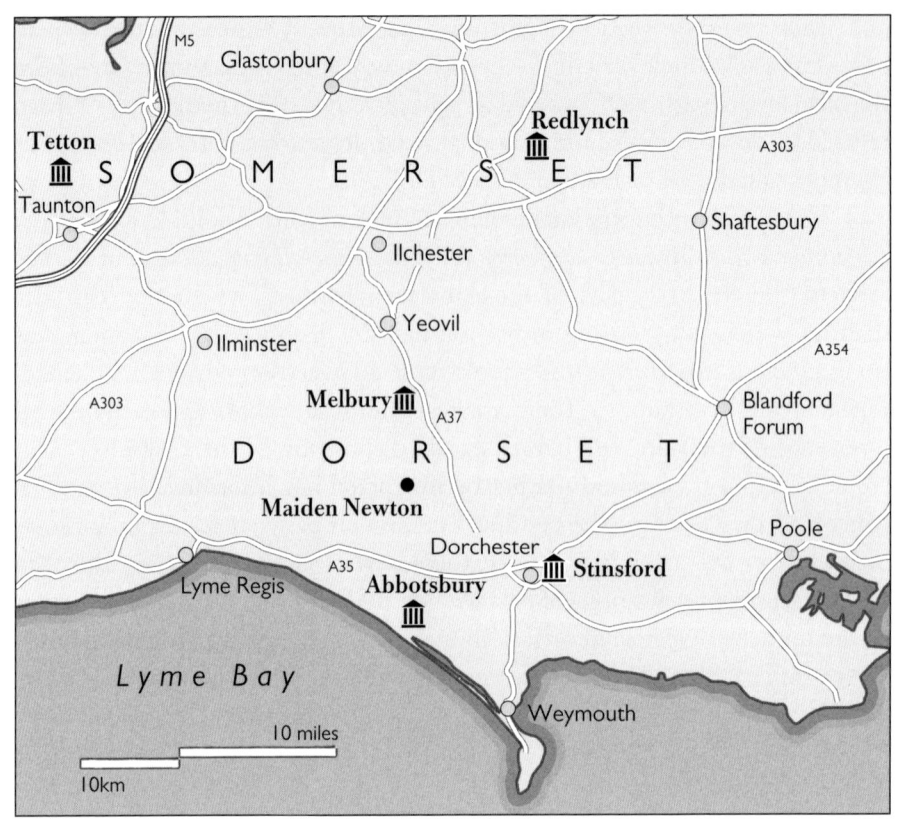

The family lands in the West Country.

PART TWO:

Attendance and Dependence

On 9 April 1787, the forty-four-year-old Lady Susan O'Brien sat in her childhood home of Redlynch, on the Somerset side of the county borders with Dorset and Wiltshire, determined 'to set down to the best of my recollection whatever of any consequence has happen'd to me for some years past'. Her idea was to produce a 'sort of History of my thoughts, plans & wishes', which for many years had had 'but one object, which was to have Mr O'B settle as a country gentleman & live within his income'. She had convinced herself that, despite appearances to the contrary, the countryside was where O'Brien would 'enjoy the greatest share of happiness'. This was largely because the couple would be socially acceptable there in a way they could never be in London.

Her rationale for making their return from North America in September 1770 the starting-point of this history was that up to that time 'all our schemes were uncertain & chang'd with every letter we received from England'. In other words, she had come to regard the moment when they defied her family's wishes by coming home without permission as the beginning of their self-determination, their attempt to map out a life of their own choosing. But she had to admit that things had not gone according to plan.

3
STINSFORD

If Susan was under any illusion that once she was back in England she would be embraced by her family as a Prodigal Daughter, she was in for a shock. For the Ilchesters the timing of her arrival could scarcely have been worse. Negotiations for the marriage of their daughter Harriot to Mr John Dyke Acland, scion of a prominent Devon family based at Killerton House near Exeter (now a National Trust property), were far advanced — and the last thing the family needed was the reappearance of this living reminder of the shame they'd had to endure over her marriage. Several years later Susan would write, 'Had I known any thing of my Sister's situation before I left [America], we should certainly have defer'd our return for another year.' She already wished she had, since coming when she did had led to a 'disagreeable altercation' between the two sisters.

She knew that her younger sister, whom she had not seen since Harriot was a child, now occupied the place she had once held in Lord Ilchester's affections and she had high hopes that the adult Harriot would act as 'an advocate with my father'. At the same time she was careful to delay writing to her until after the wedding had taken place in December 1770. But Harriot's response to her overture had dashed her hopes.

'As long as my Father remains in his present way of thinking,' Harriot had written, 'I should esteem myself unpardonable in my conduct to him did I see you in any but the privatest manner possible. I should think too, in my present situation that I became doubly culpable did I see you *now* otherwise than *Absolutely* alone. On these conditions when you come to Town I shall be glad to see you, at *your house, privately, alone & by Appointment…*'

The chilly tone of Harriot's letter, and her refusal to have anything to do with O'Brien, had enraged Susan. She fired off a stinging reply by return. 'As I never receive any company I am asham'd of,' she wrote, 'so I never intend to receive any who are asham'd of me; & as I do not commonly receive visits at my own House *privately, alone* and by *appointment* I shall not expect any of your conditional interviews.'

She dismissed as 'frivolous' the notion that her father's continuing disapproval was responsible for Harriot's standoffishness – 'My Mothers example would have authoris'd a very different behavior' – and hinted darkly at the malign influence of another family member, 'whose Head & Heart I have too much penetration not plainly to trace in this whole transaction'. Though she refrained from naming this person, it was her aunt Charlotte Digby, whom she resented for 'most unkind' treatment since her return. Even her mother had noticed it. Since her siblings adored their aunt, this sideswipe did her as little good in their eyes as the overall tenor of her attack on Harriot.

Harriot's letter and the fallout from Susan's cutting response to it, along with her father's continuing ostracism of her, and 'the mortifications of a thousand kinds, which I met with at Holland House, & which I felt more severely than any others', made this a particularly miserable time for her. Lord and Lady Holland kept her at arm's length, never inviting her to Holland House to meet old friends — as Susan noted, 'the sort of company I did meet when I was invited there were sure indications to me, who knew Lady Holland so well, that she did not wish me to be again in the world.' Reflecting on these events, particularly the row with Harriot, seventeen years later, she wrote: 'Nobody can be more susceptible of every kind of slight than I naturally am. I see & feel it in a moment, & nothing but the most unremitting attention to that fault of my temper could have corrected it so much as I think I now have done.'

Susan did manage to get herself invited to a ball at Holland House, but with a proviso that 'made it highly improper for me to have accepted' – i.e., without her husband. That was her sticking point; though she 'never could like any company but the best', she was not prepared to attend an event from which O'Brien was excluded. She told Lady Holland she had lived with him long enough to know 'that his turn of mind & conversation would be agreeable in all society'.

But though Lady Holland 'seem'd sorry', she was not to be moved. She said Lord Holland would not approve of the O'Briens living in London, since it would lead them into expense and they should avoid that above all. Besides, it was Lady Ilchester's wish that they settle in the country and she, too, thought that was the right course of action; they would be well received in any neighbourhood they chose to live in, but in London 'it was a much more difficult thing'.

Without the Hollands' support and friendship, Susan knew she would be miserable in town. In such circumstances she, too, preferred the idea of living in the country. The trouble was, the gregarious O'Brien did not. Such friends as he had independently of her were all in London and mostly in the theatre. After the years of exile in America the last thing he wanted was to be buried alive in the country where he knew no one.

At Lady Ilchester's insistence, the O'Briens had taken lodgings at Kenton Green (which was then outside London). Susan called it a 'dull place' and O'Brien characteristically expressed his opinion of it in a poem, called 'Answer to an invitation to dinner':

> You may judge my regret down at Kenton to stay
> When invited by you to a party so gay,
> Where genius assembled, mirth, friendship & ease,
> Wou'd be pleasanter far than dead bushes & trees;
> But yet my dear Major consider my case
> And I make my excuse with a very good face.
> The woman I love with an ardour unbating,
> Wou'd be my return with anxiety waiting,
> Perhaps when alone might reflect that for me
> She had fac'd ev'ry danger by Land & by Sea,
> That for me she gave up all the splendour of Life
> Contented to make a poor man's honest wife.
> Shall I leave her a moment a prey to that thought
> Which might fashion me ever to her in a fault,
> Oh no! It can't be — tho' I love all the crew
> Fitzherbert & Garrick & dearest friend, you,
> I must wa[i]ve all the joy, to my Susan I yield,
> For my Susan must conquer when once in ye field.

Though Susan heeded what Lady Holland said, the failure of a friendship she had cherished cut her to the quick: 'this absolute refusal of at all entering into my sentiments, or even making the least attempt to gratify me in my favourite wish, opened my eyes entirely to what I was to expect from this branch of my family. *Il falloit prendre parti & des ce moment je pris le mien.*'

Lord Holland, who had been ailing for some time, had grown 'almost childish' and had anyway given up on her, terminating the annuity he had paid while the O'Briens were in America and leaving them wholly dependent on Susan's mother. He told Samuel Touchet that it was hopeless trying to do anything for them, since they would do nothing for themselves.9 Any hopes of advancement that Susan now had rested on her cousin and erstwhile admirer Charles James Fox, whose political star was waxing as swiftly as his father's had waned.

Fox, who was already attracting as much attention as a 'macaroni' – a fop or dandy — and reckless gambler as he was as a politician, was rumoured to be endeavouring 'to obtain for Mr OB the Collectorship of Philadelphia', the one post that might have induced the O'Briens to go back to America. But, Susan wrote, the 'most marked neglect of me, & coolness in all our interests, was so visible in CJ's conduct' that she 'had little to hope from any exertions of his'.

Lord Ilchester had been kept in ignorance of the O'Briens' return from America for as long as possible; no one in the family had dared mention it to him. But Susan kept on pressing to see him, though when they finally did come face to face she noted sadly: 'his affection was wholly alienated from me.'

Her surprise, relief and pleasure were therefore all the greater when she discovered that as a result of a personal application from him to the prime minister Lord North, O'Brien was to get an annuity of £400 without having to go anywhere or do anything at all. The money came 'from the profits of an employment in South Carolina'. As had so often happened while they were in North America, there was talk of better things to come from the government, about which Susan was sceptical. O'Brien was less so; when she proposed that they go and live for a while more cheaply on the continent he refused to consider it, arguing that they might then miss out on some vital opportunity — or that, at least, was what he told her.

There may have been another reason for his reluctance to go abroad. Renewed contact with Drury Lane friends had inspired O'Brien to try his hand at writing for the stage — since he could no longer appear on it. He wrote just two plays. The first, a farce based on La Font's *Les trois frères rivaux* of 1713 and called *Cross Purposes*, had echoes of the popular *High Life below Stairs* (which the necrophiliac and wit George Selwyn — an habitué of

---

9 According to his *ODNB* entry, Samuel Touchet died of apoplexy on 28 May 1773, but Caroline, Lady Holland, records in her journal that on the 20th 'poor Mr Touchet hang'd himself' (BL Holland House papers, Add MSS 51444).

Holland House — had welcomed, 'For I am weary of low life above stairs'[10]). This was put on at Covent Garden by George Colman (the elder) on 5 December 1772 and was sufficiently well received to enter the repertoire; reduced to one act, it was still being performed seventy years later.

O'Brien's second play, a comedy called *The Duel*, adapted from another French piece, *Le philosophe sans le savoir*, opened at the rival Drury Lane just three days later. Garrick described it to James Boswell as 'an interesting story & very pathetick', but it failed to find favour with an audience that seems to have been swayed by a vocal minority intent on destroying it. The prompter Hopkins wrote, 'It was much hiss'd from the 2d Act & with the greatest difficulty we got thro' the Play amidst Groans hisses &c. They would not suffer it to be given out again. After many Altercations between the Audience Mr G[arrick] & Mr King[,] by the Authors Consent the Play was withdrawn.' According to Garrick's contemporary biographer Thomas Davies, 'in the opinion of good judges, [it] deserved a much better fate than it met with'.

A perusal of the script is enough to establish that *The Duel* is no lost masterpiece. The character Melville appears in the guise of a successful banker, though he is really the son of a Scottish earl whose estate had been confiscated after the Jacobite rebellion of 1715. This is obviously of biographical interest. Substitute Ireland for Scotland and Melville's background is remarkably similar to what O'Brien claimed for himself:

> … My Father was Earl of St Clair. Unhappily for him and his family he had imbibed from his Ancestors the most violent predilection for a race of Kings, whose arbitrary principles have justly been their own ruin & punishment, and involv'd in it that of their mistaken friends and supporters. In the rebellion of the year Fifteen he headed a Regiment in the service of him he thought his Prince, – the day going against them, he fled to France, leaving my mother in the greatest distress, illness, and with child, of me. Forfeiture, attainder, every calamity that can be imagined follow'd his disloyalty! he was scarcely landed when he dy'd…

Making it clear that Melville is of good birth — at the same time as mocking the exaggerated notion of family pride manifest in Melville's sister, Lady Margaret Sinclair — O'Brien indulges in further wish-fulfilment by having Melville make the fortune that was proving so elusive in his own case. If he

---

[10] After missing a visit from George Selwyn to Holland Park, the ailing Lord Holland is said to have remarked that if he were still alive the next time Selwyn called he would be delighted to see him, and if not, Selwyn (with his penchant for corpses) would be delighted to see *him*.

3 STINSFORD

hoped to achieve it as a playwright, he was disappointed. This one reverse was enough to dishearten him and put an end to a writing career that had barely begun.

※

Another factor that may have encouraged O'Brien to try his hand as a dramatist was living close to a small private theatre. He and Susan had escaped from dull Kenton Green with its 'dead bushes & trees', moving first into London and then, after they had been ostracised by Lord and Lady Holland, to Winterslow in Wiltshire, where the only member of the Fox family not to turn his back on them resided.

Ste Fox resembled — even outstripped — his younger brother Charles James in gaming and riotous living but not, alas, in political genius (in his brief and undistinguished Westminster career, hampered by deafness, he made little impression). All his short life he suffered from ill-health, starting with a form of St Vitus's Dance in infancy, from which he was never entirely cured. After three years at Eton, at the age of fourteen, a serious breakdown in health obliged him to leave the school and for the next two years he travelled with a tutor on the continent, spending the years 1760 and 1761 under the care of Dr Tronchin in Geneva. Marrying Lady Mary Fitzpatrick was one of the few things he did that pleased his father.

In the early 1760s Lord Holland had bought a 'hunting and shooting box' at Winterslow in Wiltshire (near where his father was buried), which he now had renovated and extended as a home for Ste's family. But any hope that living in the country would curb Ste's extravagance proved wide of the mark. 'The house was always full of people,' a later Lord Ilchester would write. 'He kept a pack of hounds. Hunting, shooting, and private theatricals, all helped to make the time pass pleasantly enough for his guests; but the bills increased. The plays of former days at Holland House were revived in a little theatre which Ste had added to the building…' Lady Mary's first child, a daughter named after her paternal grandmother Caroline, was born in November 1767.

Susan was drawn to Winterslow by Lady Sarah's conviction that she would find a friend in Lady Mary Fox and she did. Both Ste and Lady Mary welcomed O'Brien along with her. But they were not destined to remain there long. In the new year of 1774 the Foxes' house burned to the ground in what Lord Carlisle, in a letter to George Selwyn, aptly described as 'the first misfortune that ever happened to Stephen, which he did not bring upon himself'.

On the day before the disaster, 8 January, Ste and Lady Mary's new-born son was christened Henry Richard and in the evening two plays were performed in the little theatre at Winterslow House — *Fair Penitent* and *High Life below Stairs* (the one that had occasioned Selwyn's *bon mot* about low life above stairs). The poet Frances Greville, whose husband Fulke Greville was in the cast, stayed the night and later gave an account of the fire that broke out in the small hours of 9 January in a letter to a friend.[11] It seems to have been unconnected with the previous evening's events since there was talk of there having been a smell of smoke hanging around for one or two days beforehand. But when the flames took hold, the house had to be rapidly evacuated to avoid loss of life.

Mrs Greville offered her own Wilbury House as a refuge but Lady Pembroke got in first and 'made them go to Wilton', certainly the grandest house in those parts. Some, though, preferred to go straight back to London, whence they had come. In a letter to a mutual friend, Frances Greville pitied Lady Mary most: 'one thinks she had foreboded something bad for she had done everything in her power to prevent the play and would never rehearse once or look into her part [Lavinia in *Fair Penitent*] till the day before, & now the comfort of her life & the only place where she was happy is gone.'

The O'Briens had attended the plays but had left immediately after. (It must have been strange for O'Brien to sit through an amateur performance of the play — *High Life below Stairs* — in which he had been due to appear as Lovell at Drury Lane on the day of his clandestine marriage.) Lady Susan having gone on her own to Redlynch the next day, O'Brien found himself included in the impromptu house party at Wilton. A letter he wrote to Ste Fox a month later provides an intriguing glimpse of the once carefree actor who had always enjoyed a 'frolic in the green room'. The Earl of Pembroke arranged a visit to the theatre in Salisbury one night and among the party was a Mr Brumpton, who had played Rossano in *Fair Penitent* at Winterslow and had boasted of his bravery during the subsequent mayhem caused by the fire. O'Brien reported to Ste that they had all been sitting in an upper box, waiting for a farce to begin, when there was a fire alarm:

---

11 Frances Greville's best known poem, *A Prayer for Indifference*, was as popular in its time as Thomas Gray's *Elegy*. But her husband's gambling and jealousy of her success led to much unhappiness in her later life. Her god-daughter Fanny Burney described her as 'pedantic, sarcastic, and supercilious' – and she was an admirer.

The whole audience rose in the greatest terror & turning tail made every effort to get out — in an instant almost every one was screaming & clambering over the others back — we sat still, uncertain what it was, but Brumpton started up & made directly to the Partition that separates the Green Boxes from the Stage & most manfully pulled & tore till he had broke himself a passage thro; when I ask'd him what he was about, he swore he wou'd go thro, 'By God he would go thro'; & was with much difficulty kept from jumping down where in all probability he would have broken his neck.

Happily it turned out to be a false alarm and there was no fire. Lord Pembroke's party laughed heartily at Mr Brumpton's discomfiture and the next day, at O'Brien's instigation, they sent him a 'Bill of damages' purporting to come from the theatre manager – 'at which he swore violently & in a most furious passion sent the messenger away.' They followed this up with another impudent letter in which the manager, supposedly, wrote that 'as it was not convenient for him to pay the Bill, he would be satisfy'd if he would paint them a scene, *in the transparent way*' (suggesting both that Mr Brumpton was an artist and that they were mocking his style of painting).

Brumpton now realised that he was being set up but, far from being appeased by this, it added to his fury and he challenged O'Brien, whom he rightly held responsible for the prank, to a duel. It was only after their friends had intervened, telling him he was making an idiot of himself, that he desisted and tried to laugh off the whole thing. But being caught panicking 'on so trifling an occasion, after having boasted of so much heroism at Winterslow, has hung on his spirits exceedingly & mortify'd him ever since'.

No doubt O'Brien exaggerated the farcical elements of his story in order to amuse Ste and Lady Mary and to distract them from the private tragedy that had rendered them homeless. He could hardly have known that before the year was out a far greater one would have overtaken them.

By the end of 1774 Ste and both his parents were dead. Lord Holland, who had been ailing for so long, was the first to go and Lady Caroline survived him by a mere three weeks. She had long been suffering from cancer and willpower alone had enabled her to outlive her husband. Ste had less than six months to enjoy the title he had inherited before he, too, died (of dropsy), leaving his infant son Henry as the third to bear the name of Lord Holland within a single year.

For Susan, the 'melancholy end' of her uncle and aunt, estranged from her though they had been, could not be a matter of indifference. They had once loved her deeply and 'had from the earliest years possess'd the greatest share of my confidence & affection'. But the loss of their 'amiable friend' Ste had a more immediate impact on the O'Briens, 'as our only inducement for living at Winterslow was the pleasure of his neighbourhood'.

In December Frances Greville wrote to Lady Mary that the O'Briens were talking of 'leaving their place very soon'. She went on to say that when Lady Susan had told her she was going to her father's Burlington Street house for six weeks, she had pitied Mary, knowing 'so well how you would feel' — which suggests that Susan was pressing Mary, as the new chatelaine of Holland House, to do what Lord Holland had refused to do and invite O'Brien, along with her, to her new home. Mrs Greville continued:

> … it must be confessed however that her situation with regard to you is very distressing, tho' your good nature & perhaps a little happy insensitivity of her own may prevent in some measure her feeling it so, but, to be under a thousand obligations to anybody & to have no way of expressing ones gratitude but such as are observed to be troublesome & displeasing is… a kind of thing to make one hang oneself; I must do her the justice to say she behaved quite well the morning I was with her…

Whatever Lady Susan may have been — proud, haughty, wilful — she was certainly not insensitive; no-one was more aware of the distressing aspects of her situation than she was and if she was not prepared to satisfy the likes of Frances Greville by showing a becoming humility, that was because she knew her husband's worth and was determined to have it recognised by her peers. But Mrs Greville has form in relation to Susan. A decade earlier, in the immediate aftermath of the O'Briens' clandestine wedding, she had written Susan a letter which is worth quoting at length:

> It gave me great concern, my Dear Lady Susan, to hear that you had been informed & could believe that I should speak with severity & unkindness of you. I hoped you had been better acquainted with my heart. I know not how wrong or how right I may be with regard to the maxims of this World, but this I know that my mind has always inclined me infinitely more to the feelings of pitty than to any other sentiment when I have heard of any persons being brought by a concurrence of unlucky accidents into difficult situations & sure I cannot be less indulgent to you that I love than I could be to another; trust me my voice, tho' it is of too little consequence to do you good, shall never do you harm. You are sensible Dear Lady Susan that it is not at present possible for me to give you that mark of my good wishes for you that would be agreeable to me. This is literally the first moment that I have been able to find an

opportunity to write to you without *witnesses*. I desired Lady Sarah to beg of you to calm your mind & not to give way to unavailing sorrow because that grows at length tedious & uncomfortable to those that wish it otherwise. You will forgive my taking the liberty of offering my opinion to you. It is really because I love you to presume a little upon that degree of partiality with which you used to favour me... Adieu Dear Lady Susan, Health & Happiness attend you. May all your clouds blow over, I dare say they will, & do me the justice to rank me amongst the foremost of your Friends & well wishers.

Hmmm. Methinks the lady doth protest too much — an invitation to 'trust me' is generally a signal not to — though Susan seems to have been ready let bygones be bygones when she met her again a decade later.

Beset by the deaths of her husband and both her parents-in-law, there was little Lady Mary could now do for Susan. She herself would die four years later — of consumption. Her orphaned children, Caroline and Henry, were the taken into the care of different relations in the Duke of Bedford's family and Holland House was let for a generation. It would not be reclaimed by the family until the 3rd Lord Holland came of age and, with his ambitious wife, turned it into London's most fashionable salon.

Susan's father's coldness and her siblings' disapproval of the way she had treated Lady Harriet Acland had left Susan more than ever dependent upon her mother. Very occasionally this worked in her favour. As the sole Strangways heiress, Lady Ilchester had inherited Stinsford House, near Dorchester, on the trunk road to Exeter and points west. Traditionally, this had been the home of Strangways heirs before they came into their Melbury inheritance, but in the recent absence of male progeny it had been left uninhabited for several years and was as a consequence in a sad state of disrepair. Lady Ilchester now suggested that if it were done up a bit Susan and O'Brien might consider taking up residence there — rent-free.

The idea appealed to them both. This part of the Westcountry was home to Susan. The county town of Dorchester was only a few miles away, and the River Frome, then as now, meandered through the meadows below the house. Next door was Stinsford church. If O'Brien, who had played so many gentlemanly roles at Drury Lane, was to audition for the role of country gentleman in real life, where better to do it than at Stinsford? He was much taken with the setting and eager to give it a try, going so far as to consult with Lady Sarah, who had some 'very pretty spaniels' and a brother, the Duke of Richmond, 'famous for pointers', on what would be the most suitable dogs for them to have (they settled for two spaniels, one of which – 'Poor dear Fop' – lived with them for twelve years).

For Susan the appeal of Stinsford, neglected though it was, was irresistible: 'the place was exceptionally pretty, & the spot in the Kingdom I prefer'd as a residence.' It was a substantial, if not particularly beautiful country house (in his poem, Hardy has Su describe it as 'our grey hall') – big enough to be divided into several dwellings in the late twentieth century. As it belonged to her family, she hoped that her occupation of it would bring about at least a partial reconciliation with her brothers and sisters. 'What reasons then,' she asked herself, 'were there to make me doubt the propriety of going there?' Her answer: 'Mr O'B's disposition to expence, & my Mother's total incapacity for business.'

O'Brien's extravagance had already caused her considerable embarrassment and the debts they had accrued in America were not paid off until 1773, three years after they had left the country, and then only by means of a gift of £2,000 from Lady Ilchester. But Susan managed to persuade herself that for O'Brien 'a change of situation might make a change of disposition'. She conceded this was 'the weakest of all imaginations' but clung to the hope that having obtained what he wanted he would 'see the necessity of economy to preserve it'.

As for her mother, her lack of business sense was such that she believed £50 would suffice to make the house habitable — a figure that Lord Ilchester's steward, Mr Donisthorpe, regarded as ludicrous, saying the true cost would be nearer £1,500. But Lady Ilchester, who wanted her childless eldest daughter near at hand now that Lord Ilchester's health was uncertain (after an attack of palsy shortly before his brother's death) and she herself was ageing, insisted the work go ahead. The work was carried out in a piecemeal fashion, with no builder consulted or plan made.

The O'Briens moved in during the summer of 1775, despite the fact that 'by the extreme of bad management after £1,000 had been laid out, it is still so out of repair, as to be unfit either to let, or to inhabit'. Yet such was their desire for a home of their own that Susan wrote, 'we came to it with the greatest satisfaction imaginable. I had lost all my apprehensions & fears of future consequences in the joy of coming to live in Dorsetshire; in having pleas'd both Mr O'B & my Mother by doing so, & in having a prospect of being fix'd for Life...'

1. *(above)* **Lord Hervey and his Friends** by William Hogarth (*c.* 1742). Stephen Fox is seated at the table; his brother Henry Fox is standing to the right of him, holding up a drawing of a building, to which Lord Hervey is gesturing.

2. *(right)* The young Stephen Fox, 1st Lord Ilchester, with gun and dead bird, suitably for a man who avoided London as much as he could, preferring country life and sports (artist unknown).

3. Katherine Read's portrait of Lady Susan (1764). Charles James Fox called it 'not only an excellent picture, but the best likeness that I think has ever been taken of her'.

4. *(facing page)* Lady Sarah Lennox (leaning out of the casement), Charles James Fox and Lady Susan Fox-Strangways by Sir Joshua Reynolds (c. 1762), a picture hated by Susan, who wrote that while 'C Fox was a spirited good likeness, Lady Sarah and I were disfigured & insipid (which we were not)'.

Lady Susan's Unsuitable Marriage

5. David Garrick and his friends, an engraving after Hogarth (who sits with his back to us in the foreground pointing at Garrick); William O'Brien, holding a stick, is seated on the right of the main group, nearest to Garrick's outstretched arm. Henry Woodward, the man he replaced at Drury Lane, is third from the left in the back row.

6. Lady Sarah as Almeria in Congreve's *The Mourning Bride*, a pastel by Katherine Read, *c.*1764.

7. Ste Fox (later, 2nd Lord Holland), a pastel by Katherine Read, 1765.

Lady Susan's Unsuitable Marriage

8. *(right)* Lady Susan Fox-Strangways aged 18, painted by Allan Ramsay in 1761.

9. *(below)* Susan's younger brother Henry Thomas, 2nd Earl of Ilchester, whose gaming rivalled that of his cousins Ste and Charles James Fox, painted by Thomas Beach in 1778.

10. *(right)* Charles James Fox at the age of 45 painted by Karl Anton Hickel in 1794.

11. Southern view of New York City from across the East River in the 1760s.

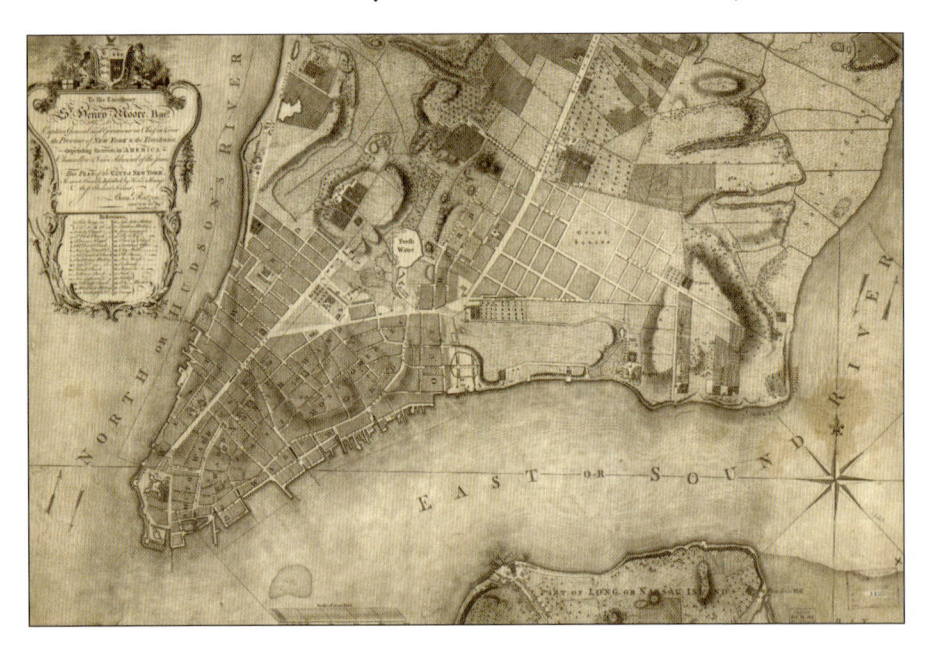

12. Bernard Ratzer's *Plan of the City of New York*, 1769.

LADY SUSAN'S UNSUITABLE MARRIAGE

13. Johnson Hall: Sir William Johnson presenting medals to the Indian Chiefs of the Six Nations at Johnstown, NY, 1772. This oil painting, by Edward Lamson Henry (1903), is a suspiciously orderly and sanitised rendering of reality.

14. Stinsford in the 21st century. Lady Susan loved her Dorset home, but her constant fear of losing it meant she was seldom at ease there. The house is now divided into several dwellings.

13. William O'Brien and Lady Susan in two pastels by Francis Cotes from the early 1760s. Susan wrote that Cotes had considered the picture of O'Brien his 'masterpiece' and had intended it for the Royal Academy. But it was the cause of great anxiety to her both in the early days of her marriage and again in her widowhood.

3 STINSFORD

Lady Susan's father died in the autumn of 1776. Her sadness that her father should have died still estranged from her was modified by two considerations: his death removed the greatest obstacle to a family reconciliation; and it presaged a change in her fortune. Her mother, she found, had never been more determined to 'make a provision for us'. Aware that her own income was only for life, Lady Ilchester gave them £100 a year in addition to the £200 annuity Lord Ilchester had — at her insistence — left them, along with the £2,500 'younger child's fortune' to which Susan (the oldest, but a daughter) was entitled. This amounted to 'a tolerable income' and one that was increased by another £100 a year in 1777, when Lady Ilchester let them have part of Stinsford Farm rent-free. O'Brien had been keen to acquire this land, for though he had no bent for farming, in his role as country gentleman it 'afforded him some amusement as well as profit'.

All might have been well but for O'Brien's 'disposition to expence', which the occupation of Stinsford House only exacerbated. The O'Briens' circle of acquaintance, which was 'both numerous & agreeable', consisted of people much richer than themselves, such as their close neighbours the Pitts at Kingston Maurward. William Morton Pitt — a cousin of William Pitt the younger, as Susan was of Charles James Fox, Pitt's great rival — was an MP for the county of Dorset. Though some years younger than the O'Briens, he and his wife Margaret became their closest friends in the country. Susan pleaded with O'Brien not to attempt to compete with such people in providing lavish entertainment. She argued that 'the greater people were, the less they expected it or enjoy'd it in others' – and especially from them, whose situation was widely known. But in vain: no matter how often she remonstrated with him, O'Brien found it impossible to economise. Though their circumstances had improved, the war that had broken out in America had put an end to the £400 annuity that her father had obtained for them from Lord North.

The American war was much in the news. Lady Sarah praised Susan for her *prévoyance* over it: 'do you remember all *your* rebellious letters from America ten years ago? I see your spirit is not lessened on that subject, nor can I wonder at it, for without having any partiality for America, I grow a greater rebel every day upon principle.' In that respect, as in her politics generally, Lady Sarah followed Charles James Fox, who led the opposition to the war for which he blamed her erstwhile suitor, George III. In a reference to what might have been, Sarah told Susan she thanked God that she was not queen, since 'I should certainly go mad, to think a person I loved was the cause of such a shameful war'.

O'Brien also felt passionately on the subject and wrote supportively to Charles Fox, who thanked him for information that 'tallied exactly with all I have heard from Philadelphia'. Fox deplored the fact that the 'very Government which has confessedly ruined the country, is as strong as ever'. As for his own prospects, the best Charles could hope for was to be 'thought well of,' which was the 'only reward to be expected of those who will not make themselves absolute tools to the ruling powers of the country'. Should he ever become as great as O'Brien hoped he might be, his 'greatest comfort' would be 'the power of serving those who have not been ashamed of declaring themselves my friends in the worst times'. Such sentiments did him credit, but were they worth any more than his promises to repay the huge loans his friends had provided to settle his gambling debts?

Susan's interest in the war was personal as well as political. Two of her siblings were caught up in the conflict: her second brother Stephen Strangways was a captain in the 24th (2nd Warwickshire) Regiment of Foot; and her estranged sister Lady Harriot had taken the highly unusual step (for an officer's wife) of accompanying her husband, now a major in the 20th (East Devonshire) of Foot, to America, leaving her two infant daughters in her mother's care. Coincidentally, both men were wounded on the same day, 7 October 1777, on Bemis Heights at Saratoga, in the battle that tipped the scales of the war in favour of the colonialists, bringing the French in on the American side. John Dyke Acland's wounds were more serious than Strangways's. He had been shot through both legs and, being unable to run away, had fallen into enemy hands. This brought out the best in Lady Harriot, whose actions earned her a footnote in history (and an entry in the *Oxford Dictionary of National Biography*).

Two days after the battle, Harriot persuaded the defeated English General Burgoyne to provide a *laissez-passer* for her to cross over into enemy territory, where she planned to nurse her wounded husband back to health. The fact that she was pregnant for a third time did not deter her from undertaking a risky night journey down the Hudson River in a rowing boat with only her maid, her husband's valet (also wounded) and the army chaplain,

Rev. Edward Brudenell, carrying a white flag, for company. Legend has it that when she arrived at an enemy outpost late at night in an open boat, she and her small party were not permitted to land. The American sentries suspected a ruse and kept the party waiting until daybreak, by which time Lady Harriot was supposedly 'half dead with anxiety and terror'. Though General Burgoyne — for reasons of his own — put this story about, his earliest report merely states that 'Lady Acland's boat reached the American outpost at about ten o'clock at night, whereupon she hailed the sentries herself and was taken to Major Dearborn's log cabin on shore until meeting General Gates the following morning'. This less dramatic version (and John Burgoyne would enjoy more success as a playwright than as a general) seems to have been nearer the truth.

Horatio Gates, Burgoyne's opposite number, received Harriot courteously and provided her with an escort to take her to her husband, who was already being transported to the military hospital in the American base at Albany. A further two months would pass before Acland was able to stand again — two months in which mutual respect and affection grew between the Aclands and Gates and his officers. In a letter to his wife, Gates would describe Lady Harriot as 'the most amiable, delicate little piece of Quality you ever beheld' and though he called the major a 'most confounded Tory', he joked that he was not without hope of converting him into a Whig.[12]

On hearing the news of Harriot's exploit, Lady Sarah wrote to Susan, 'I do pity Lady Harriot most truly, & yet am convinced the *spirit* you all possess makes her a compleat heroine & above female distresses...' The exchange of prisoners at Christmas enabled the Aclands to return to England and with Susan spending much of her time with her mother at Melbury, it was inevitable that the estranged sisters would soon come face to face. When that

---

[12] In the House of Commons on 26 October 1775 the youthful John Dyke Acland had been entrusted by Lord North with opening the debate on the escalation of the American war. Acland had concluded his rousing speech to fellow MPs with a rhetorical question: 'Shall we be told then that these people [American rebels], whose greatness is the work of our hands, and whose insolence arises from our divisions, who have mistaken the lenity of this country for weakness, and the reluctance to punish for a want of power to vindicate the rights of British subjects – shall we be told that such a people can resist the powerful effects of this nation?' (cited in David McCullough, *1776: America and Britain at War*, p. 14). Then, putting his money where his mouth was, he went off to fight for King and Country.

After Acland's release and return to England, George III sent for him in order to hear his account of the battle of Saratoga and to encourage him to resume his seat in the Commons. But there is no record of his having spoken there again. So perhaps Horatio Gates was more successful than he imagined in making Acland think again.

happened, Susan was happy to record that 'every thing was made up'. Unfortunately, John Dyke Acland never fully recovered from 'the wounds and other ill effects of His Campaign in America'. He died in November 1778 after catching a chill when fighting an early morning duel (over a trifle) in which neither party was injured. He was in his early thirties and the twenty-eight-year-old Harriot, who had given birth to their only son in February of that year, was left a widow with three young children.

Though Susan hardly knew her brother-in-law, for her too, his death was a grievous loss; 'had he lived,' she wrote, 'I have no doubt I sh^d have had in him a valuable & zealous friend — for the warm & active disposition he was of, when once it professes regard, is generally found to be the most sincere & generous friend.'

4
THE DYE IS CAST

Lady Susan's reconciliation with her family now complete, she could enjoy a sense of belonging that, crucially for her, included O'Brien, since he too was now accepted by them all. But just when everything seemed to be falling into place — at least as far as Susan was concerned — domestic harmony was threatened as never before. In fifteen years of marriage, no matter what pressures they had laboured under, both in exile and on their unheralded return, Susan and William had supported each other to the utmost — indeed, adversity seemed only to strengthen the bond between them. But now Susan saw ominous signs of a growing restlessness in O'Brien.

The novelty of being a country gentleman had soon worn off and, galvanised by events in America and the opposition to the war led by Charles James Fox, he yearned to take a more active part in public affairs. So long as he was dabbling in politics, speaking out on the subject of the American war at a public meeting, for instance, Susan was not overly concerned — though she feared he would be disappointed in his hopes of being rewarded for his loyalty to her cousin Charles. It was only when his dreams of success in public life crystallised into a scheme of becoming a barrister that she became alarmed.

Ever since marriage to Susan had obliged him to give up his chosen profession, O'Brien had nursed hopes of training for another which would make use of his proven skills as a performer. Reporting their departure from London to America in September 1764, the *Gazetteer & New Daily Advertiser* had noted O'Brien's intention of becoming a lawyer — which, if true, formed no part of the long discussions of their future that he and Susan had had with Lord Holland's advisers. Had anyone dared raise the idea with his lordship, there can be no doubt it would have been given short shrift on the grounds of expense.

O'Brien had been a young man then, still in his twenties, and had their circumstances allowed, he might well have been able to fulfil his ambition. But he was nearly forty when he broke the news to Susan that he had made up his mind to train for the law at Lincoln's Inn. Frustrated by repeated failures to find any satisfying employment or occupation, he was determined to do this before it was too late. He tried to persuade Susan that this was their best chance of breaking free of financial dependence on her increasingly capricious mother, arguing that once he had qualified he would at last be able to earn enough money to give them the independence they craved.

But Susan was unconvinced. She thought it was already too late, and his health too uncertain, for him to undertake the necessary study. She had no doubt he might have done it once, but that moment had passed. She also believed he was deluding himself in imagining it would be a good investment. Even if he survived the rigours of intensive study and qualified as a barrister, by the time he got to that point the expenditure involved — not least in living in London — would have used up their meagre resources. The prospect of her father's legacy disappearing on such a doomed project was more than she could bear. For the first time in their life together they were not united in the face of an uncomprehending and hostile world, but divided one against the other. Susan had the stronger will, but O'Brien could be very stubborn. He had made up his mind; and, to her surprise and annoyance, he had gained the support of other members of her family, from whom she expected more sense.

Susan responded by refusing to accompany him to London, nominally on the grounds of expense — it would cost less if he went on his own. Besides, she had her widowed mother to consider, as well as him. At Stinsford, she was well placed to receive visiting members of her family, as well as friends, on their way to and from Melbury and, during the summer months, to Abbotsbury, where her mother had built herself a house by the sea — or to Weymouth, where the seasonal presence of royalty acted as a magnet. For family and social reasons, then, as well as her abiding love of the place, she was utterly averse to the idea of leaving Stinsford.

O'Brien, on the other hand, childless and now middle-aged, too long an appendage of his wife and debarred from pursuing a promising career on the stage, was set on making one last bid for independence and self-fulfilment. As a barrister-at-law he saw himself cutting a dash in court, just as he had once done on stage, for the two professions, no matter how different their social status, had in common a strong element of public performance; and if he struck it out, he might also achieve the fame and fortune he still craved. On this occasion even Susan, to whose judgment he was generally happy to defer, was powerless to change his mind.

4 THE DYE IS CAST

O'Brien began his first term at Lincoln's Inn in February 1781, while Susan was languishing at Bath with her mother. He wrote to his 'sweet Nett' – who was feeling anything but sweet — that he had seen Charles Fox, who had been as supportive of his career move as everybody else, including her brother Henry Thomas, now Lord Ilchester, had been. One thing was becoming increasingly clear to him, though: 'I *must* give up the country.' Susan would have to 'muster up resolution to do what is absolutely necessary & proper to be done', and put the best possible face on it to her mother; there could be no half-measures about this: 'The dye is cast…' By stressing the economic benefits of a career as a barrister, he hoped to win over Susan to his point of view. But the strain was already beginning to tell on him. Honesty forced him to admit that he 'had not been so well today as I was yesterday'. He ended his letter touchingly: 'I long to shew the world, I am worthy of you.'

Susan hardly knew how to respond. On the one hand, she 'did not like to contradict an inclination that had then such possession of Mr O'B's mind'; on the other, her heart revolted 'to a degree I can scarcely imagine' at the prospect of giving up Stinsford and living in London. She resolved that 'tho I might acquiesce I wd never approve what wd make me miserable & in a very short time I was convinced must plunge Mr OB into all sorts of difficultys'. And she refused point-blank to leave Stinsford 'in the present state of the business'.

O'Brien's next letter showed Susan just how hard a time he was having. He told her he had been 'fagging all day': in the morning at Westminster Hall, listening to a lot of stuff he didn't even begin to understand; and in the afternoon he had spent four hours at the Serjeants' Chambers in Chancery Lane copying out 'several sheets of Precedents of Actions' in trespass cases. 'Such is the life I lead.'

As he had promised always to let her know how he was, he also had to admit that he was in a bad way physically, never sleeping more than three hours at a stretch and frequently having to get up in the night to relieve the pain in his back. He looked well enough, as the doctor he had consulted told him was often the case with nervous complaints. The doctor's recommendation was that he take the waters at Spa (in what is now Belgium) and, failing that, be treated by electricity, which he had never found to be of the slightest use. 'As to my pursuit,' he went on, knowing full well what Susan would be thinking, 'I am convinced that does not hurt me; it occupies me; and so far is a good rather than an evil.'

Susan poured out her troubles to Sarah. But Sarah had other things on her mind just then. She wrote to Susan on 14 May 1781, announcing that she was intending to marry again, though she knew it was against her interest to lose the protection of a kind — and wealthy — brother. She was in love, and the object of her affection was a widowed army officer (with a daughter), Colonel George Napier, a tall and strikingly handsome but impoverished younger son of a Scottish baron and his Irish wife.[13]

She sympathised with Susan over the prospect of living in London again. 'You say I know how London *was* & *will be* to you,' she wrote: 'I know it still better for myself, but my part is taken long ago on that score, & the only advantage upon earth I have over you, is, that I can bend my disposition to *any* thing that is necessary, which you cannot. I admire your tough, *oaklike* mind, but I avail myself of my own weakness & at least take the good of it, since I have suffered by the bad of such a bending, pliant turn of mind.' A retired life suited her well and she would continue to lead such a life, whether in London or in the country; it made no difference to her; she had given up the world 'upon sound and fair reasoning, & no temptation shall ever make me seek it again'. For Susan it was different: she had no children and the reading and other occupations that filled her life in the country would not satisfy her in London, especially with O'Brien so entirely taken up with his studies. Hence, Sarah concluded, 'you will have no resource but in society for which you are formed by nature' (but from which she was excluded).

Sarah wished O'Brien 'much better luck than I think he will have', but she couldn't blame him for taking a risk, since she was doing the same: 'we both play a deep game, I hope we shall not meet with ruin, but with happiness...'

Sarah's news came as a bombshell to Susan, who replied that though she'd intended to do no more than to wish her happiness, she couldn't help feeling 'hurt' at her marrying again: 'there was a propriety in yr retreat, & a dignity annex'd to the idea of *one great passion*, tho' unfortunately placed, that gratified your friends & silenced your enemies.' She offered her advice, and worried that the change in Sarah's status would affect her daughter Louisa, who was used to having her undivided attention.

---

[13] Napier and Lady Sarah would go on to have a large number of children together – including three brothers who all fought in the Peninsular War and became generals, and another who became an admiral. The eldest, Charles James Napier (named after C.J. Fox), had a particularly distinguished – if controversial – military career.

But her main concern was over money. 'I am sorry,' she wrote, 'if you will marry, that it is a man of small fortune… neither time or habit, that lessens every other ill, has the least effect on this.' She was speaking from bitter experience; she was, after all, something of an expert on the subject. 'There is a perpetual little uneasiness occasion'd by the want of money,' she went on (in a manner reminiscent of her contemporary, Jane Austen); 'a little something which arises every day, & every day wants a fresh remedy, like the continued pricking of a pin, tho' no very violent agony yet enough to make one's whole life uncomfortable.'

Even so, it was her most ardent wish that her dear Lady Sarah should be 'as happy as the lot of humanity will allow'.

Her own predicament was unchanged. O'Brien remained in London and she with her mother, now at Melbury 'surrounded by oaks'. Yet she assured Sarah she had 'nothing of the *oaklike* disposition you imagine'. She had become more of 'a willow & very often a weeping one, for my spirits are but low, & I can't form any scheme for this law situation that affords me any pleasure even in imagination'.

Her desperation is evident from the fact that, without telling O'Brien, she swallowed her — very considerable — pride and wrote a heartfelt letter to her cousin Charles, begging him to use his political influence to get her husband a place — a letter that suffered the fate of most begging letters (not just those addressed to Charles James Fox) and went unanswered.

※

The beginning of 1784 saw both the O'Briens living in London in a house they'd rented in Lincoln's Inn Fields to enable O'Brien to launch his career as a barrister. But he was so ill that it seemed to Susan 'almost madness… to persevere in a pursuit that had so little prospect of success, & the expense of which we could not support, even long enough to give it a trial'.

O'Brien's usually equable temper had deteriorated along with his health. 'He became tenacious & obstinate,' Susan wrote, '& would not endure the least contradiction, or even difference of opinion… Tho he could not pass a night without opium, or a day without the most excruciating pain, he would attend Westminster Hall & was determin'd to go [on] the Spring Circuits.'

They went to Stinsford and met up with the judges at Dorchester, but O'Brien was too ill to go further. Nor did he get any better when they returned to London. Susan was utterly miserable – 'every thing I most apprehended was by visible steps rapidly approaching me: Mr OB's health quite gone; his Life in great danger; our little fortune disappearing so fast, that if he did live, it would soon be so reduced as not to afford him the comforts conveniences & attendance that ill health always requires, & which being accustomed to were now become absolutely necessary to him.'

The crisis came in the summer. O'Brien once again joined the western circuit. He reached Exeter on Monday 2 August, having been taken ill on the road between Bridport, where he'd dined, and Axminster, where he'd spent a miserable evening and sleepless night. Though he was now feeling a little better, he wrote pathetically to his dear sweet Nett, 'I am afraid you are growing to hate me, for join'd to my old imperfections, I feel I have too many new peevish intolerable ways that I am made miserable by thinking you feel me not the person you once liked.' He assured her he still loved her – 'if possible more than I ever did' – and worried what would become of him if she could no longer put up with him.

He collapsed again in Exeter and, though he staggered on to Bristol, he could not continue. Susan's brother Henry Thomas, 2nd Earl of Ilchester, accompanied her there to fetch him. They got back to Redlynch on 24 August and immediately summoned the doctor. Mr Samson did not expect him to survive many hours — so was surprised to learn that he'd dined and supped with the family. Susan described what happened next:

> But in going upstairs at night [he] fainted away, & continued repeatedly to do so every time he moved the next day. The following one, he could not get up at all, & growing hourly weaker & weaker, was in the night of the 26th absolutely given over; Mr Samson standing by his bedside & expecting every breath would be his last — but the goodness of his constitution, & the skill & unremitted care of Mr Samson, got over this dreadfull crisis, & in some days there were hopes he might recover.

Susan had been aware for some time that O'Brien had become indifferent to life. His poor health, his thwarted ambition and the 'embarrass'd situation of his affairs prey'd on his mind', so that death seemed more desirable than fearful to him. 'I *think* he did wish for it,' she wrote. 'I *know* I fear'd it.' She was troubled by the thought that she might be guilty of placing her own happiness above his in longing and praying that he might survive when she didn't believe he would ever again enjoy good health.

During the O'Briens' stay in her childhood home Susan received 'many proofs of my Brother & Lady Ilchester's kindness & attention; & I feel for them the strong tye of gratitude added to every other that connects us'. Their generosity was one of the two bonuses to come out of this severe trial as far as Susan was concerned. The other was that for O'Brien it was certain to bring about 'a total change in his intentions & future plan of Life'. He couldn't possibly go on with a scheme that had placed not just his health but his very life in jeopardy.

After a month at Redlynch, O'Brien was well enough in body, if not in spirit, to make the journey back to Stinsford. The crisis might have passed, but there would be a long period of recovery — including six months of recuperation at Spa they could ill afford — before he showed so much as a glimmer of his earlier zest for life.

In her retrospective account of the years between 1770 and 1787, Susan does not give any indication that she ever wondered whether her opposition towards O'Brien's cherished law scheme might not have contributed to its ultimate failure. Heaven knows, it was a hard enough challenge for him without his wife's all-too-evident scepticism over his chances of bringing it off. In the early days of their marriage, when Susan had been driven to the edge of despair by the sharpness of her family's rejection, it was only O'Brien's steady and affectionate support that had kept her going. Yet now, in his hour of greatest need, she could be said to have lacked 'faith' in him (just as her fictional *alter ego* in Thomas Hardy's 'The Noble Lady's Tale' does); she did not believe he would succeed. He'd had to go it alone in the teeth of her opposition — and even then he had almost made it.

※

The cost of O'Brien's legal education and living in London had frittered away the inheritance from Susan's father and left them more than ever financially dependent on the Dowager Lady Ilchester. This, combined with their childlessness, meant that Susan's wealthy siblings tended to take it for granted that she should always be at her mother's beck and call as a kind of superior servant, or 'lady companion', rather than an equal.

Lady Ilchester liked to spend Christmas and New Year at Discove, a spartan farmhouse close to Redlynch. At the beginning of 1789 she chose to extend her stay there, with the O'Briens in attendance, until the end of April. This was an ordeal for them both, as Susan recorded in her journal: 'My Mother whose complaints increase, & whose temper was never an easy one, is now become so difficult to live with, that hardly a day has pass'd without disputes, or marks of displeasure of some kind or other.' O'Brien kept to his room as much as he could and avoided playing cards, since that 'fertile source of ill humour', as Susan characterised it, invariably led to rows. The trouble was, cards had become the old lady's sole occupation and Susan frequently had to humour her by playing for up to eight hours a day.

'I feel myself almost unequal to my situation,' she wrote, '& dread the idea of leaving Mr OB in total dependance on a capricious mind. I have long suffer'd the misery of it. I have never been deceiv'd. I saw the effect on others in my earliest years, & dreaded it. I have done every thing in *my* power to keep myself & Mr OB from it, but all my efforts have fail'd, & no one can more than I do, feel the curse *of attendance & dependance*.'

By the end of the year – 'as unpleasant a one in every respect' as she had ever experienced — Susan was 'tired to death'. Nothing but the thought of how awful it would be for O'Brien if she predeceased her mother could induce her 'to endure another year of such ennui, uneasiness, & fear'. Yet for all the monotony of living with mother at Melbury, or at the seaside house she had recently had built for herself at Abbotsbury, or at Discove, the endless carping and card-playing, she was only too aware that spending half the year there was what enabled them to live the other half at Stinsford without sinking hopelessly into debt.

This double — or half — life of summers at Stinsford, to which her attachment had 'almost become a passion', and winters at Discove or Melbury continued for a further year and a half. During the first six months of 1792, in which Lady Ilchester remained at Melbury and demanded constant attendance, Susan watched her 'visible decline' with increasing alarm, not least because of the continuing uncertainty of what would become of her and O'Brien without her support. Yet the old lady hung on through the summer and into the autumn, lulling Susan into a false sense of security.

The suddenness of her mother's death on 15 October took everyone by surprise. To the very end Lady Ilchester had come downstairs daily and gone through her usual routines, '& even on the last day did not seem to suffer pain' – though she'd suffered a great deal of it in her rheumatic old age. Given the amount of time Susan had spent at her side, it is ironic that she should have been absent at the crucial moment. She hurried to Melbury as soon as she got word that her mother was dying but still arrived too late to see her alive.

However strained their relationship had become, her loss was a severe one. Yet Susan reflected proudly that her mother had been served 'with zeal & fidelity' by all about her: 'There never were *more Old* & affectionate servants, who had lived so long together in any House, & never more real sorrow & grief at the breaking up of any family.'

But after all she'd done for her mother Susan found she was to be left 'almost as dependant as ever', and once again made to feel the precariousness of her situation. She had had little in the way of expectations but was horrified to discover 'that little so shackled, & embarrass'd, as to be thrown instantly dependant on my Brother, to live here even in or out of England, as his generosity or affection may dispose'. Lord Ilchester's generally easy-going manner with the O'Briens would change once they became dependent on him. Susan believed he meant well, but he was so cold and distant towards her that she found it impossible to discuss with him all the things that needed to be done at Stinsford and relied on her sister Harriot to act as her advocate (as she had once hoped Harriot might have been with her father).

Now widowed and with five growing daughters who would have to be presented at court and given a London season to mark their entry into society's marriage market, Susan's brother had more urgent matters on his mind than his eldest sister's lack of the wherewithal to maintain her chosen way of life. His own rakish lifestyle did not help. He had fathered two illegitimate children, a son and a daughter, during his marriage; and his eldest (legitimate) daughter Lady Elizabeth would recall a telling childhood encounter with her father at their London house in Burlington Street. She and her sister Lady Mary were about to be taken on their morning walk when he returned from an all-night gambling session very much the worse for wear. The little girls ran up to embrace him, only to be roughly brushed aside.

In his youth Henry Thomas Fox-Strangways (during his father's lifetime known as Lord Stavordale) had acquired a reputation for gaming and debauchery which rivalled that of his cousins Ste and Charles James Fox. In 1770 Horace Walpole had described the prevalence of gaming among aristocratic young men as 'worthy the decline of an Empire', noting that they would lose anything from five to fifteen thousand pounds in a single evening. He wrote that Lord Stavordale, who had yet to come of age, 'lost eleven thousand last Tuesday, but recovered it by one great hand at hazard. He swore a great oath — "Now, if I had been playing deep, I might have won millions!"'

Older but no wiser, his addiction to gambling proved less profitable, and by the 1790s the parlous state of his finances had reached the ears of George III. In conversation with one of Susan's Dorset friends, Mrs Lionel Damer, on one of his regular summer visits to Weymouth, the King remarked that he'd heard Lord Ilchester had 'hurt his fortune much, & was in distress'd circumstances'.

Her brother's inability or unwillingness to help, along with the seeming impossibility of finding employment for O'Brien, despite the good intentions of their circle of friends, made the 1790s a decade of ever-increasing anxiety for Susan. In June 1794 she had a rare opportunity to see her dearest friend Lady Sarah, most of whose life was now spent in Ireland with her growing (in both sense of the word) family. They met at Southampton where Sarah's husband Col. Napier was briefly stationed. The two women, united in adversity as they had once been in good fortune, enjoyed comparing their situations – 'tho unable to assist each other in essentials, yet the pleasure of really free & confidential conversation is very great, especially after being deprived of it as I have been.' With others Susan had to watch what she said in case of appearing to be complaining, or 'intimating discontents or wants – even my Sister's goodness to me has been such that I cannot help feeling that talking to her again of my difficultys is like asking her again to help'.

It was not long since Harriot's daughter Kitty had come to Susan's rescue with an 'unexpected mark of kindness & affection' in the form of a gift of £500. But this act of extraordinary generosity was in stark contrast to the behaviour of Lord Ilchester. Far from helping to improve her situation, in 1797 he made it worse by taking over the leasing of Stinsford farm and thus depriving the O'Briens of nearly £200 annual income. Susan called that 'a most bitter pill'. But it was nothing compared to the crisis she would have to face before the end of this unhappy decade.

PART THREE:

Darby and Joan

'The patient being placed in a chair of convenient height, in a reclining posture, her head supported with a pillow, by an assistant behind, and her arms secured by another on each side, the Surgeon is... to make one horizontal incision, longer than the diseased mass, nearly in the direction of the rib, and a little below the nipple... The most painful part of the operation being over, the assistants... are now to... press their fingers on any arteries that bleed freely, which will enable the surgeon... to remove the whole of the diseased mass, which should be carefully dissected from the skin above, and below from the pectoral muscle and ribs...

Over the sutures and adhesive plaister, a large, thick, soft, compress of old linen should be applied, and gently bound on, with a flannel roller, about five inches broad, and six or eight yards long... The serous or bloody discharge is generally in such quantity as to appear through all the bandages...'

— *(Henry Fearon,* A Treatise on Cancers, with a New and Succesful Method of Operating, Particularly in Cancers of the Breast and Testis, *1784)*

5
A Dreadful Malady

Susan's constant concern over O'Brien's health meant that she gave little thought to her own. She had a robust constitution and enjoyed an active life. But in the spring of 1798, when she was in her mid-fifties, she became aware of a physical symptom that she could not ignore, hard though she tried. The lump on her breast, though it gave her no pain, did not go away. The physician she consulted, Adair Hawkins, who was also a friend, recommended treatments — applying leeches and taking hot baths — she found as ineffective as she had feared they would be. But when he gently suggested she might consider surgery, adding that he was not 'an advocate for operations of the *Knife*' if they could be avoided, she recoiled in horror, saying she had 'little confidence in the success of such experiments'.

Susan was a strong woman but she doubted she could summon up the courage to submit to the knife. Her brother Lord Ilchester and his second (and much younger) wife Maria, née Digby, both urged her to go to London so she could get the best opinions, to which end they offered her the use of their Burlington Street house. Grateful though she was, she still resisted the notion of seeing a surgeon, 'who has but one thing to propose, & that too terrible to bear the thought of'. Before the development of anaesthetics the prospect of being sliced open and diseased matter cut or scraped away while remaining fully conscious was indeed horrific. To avoid such a fate she was even prepared to put herself in the hands of a so-called healer, of whom she had heard good reports — though she reproached herself for such weakness: 'How foolish this is! to prefer ignorance & an old woman's nonsense to science, skill, & good sense. Yet I can not help it...' At least this got her to London, where Mrs Hobson, the woman who had been recommended to her, lived.

She and O'Brien did not go to 31 Burlington Street but stayed with her cousin and brother-in-law, Stephen Digby, in Richmond, where Digby held the post of Ranger and Keeper of the Royal Park. Although this was convenient, it may not have been an ideal place for her to stay. Her cousin had married her favourite sister, Lady Lucy, the one nearest to her in age, who had died a decade earlier — of breast cancer.

She went to see Mrs Hobson on 14 December, having first consulted Adair Hawkins and Sir Walter Farquhar, Physician-in-Ordinary to the Prince of Wales, who agreed it could no her no harm (if not much good either). Mrs Hobson duly told her what she wanted to hear, namely that her complaint was not so bad, and gave her 'medicines' she claimed would soon put her right. Susan did her best to keep up her hopes that these nostrums would work, but by February 1799 her confidence was waning: 'the longer I stay & am under Mrs Hobson's care without success, the more I fear to have other advice given me, that I shall be neither willing or able to take.'

At the end of March she saw a doctor strongly recommended by her sister Harriot, who had come to London to give her support. Though he gave her advice she welcomed, to go into the country for a few months of peace and quiet and then consult him again, she found it odd that he should regard her case as so much less urgent than the other doctors she'd consulted had. So she went back to see Adair Hawkins, who strongly opposed the idea of her leaving London. On his advice, which was echoed by her friends, she finally agreed to see the eminent surgeon, Charles Blicke.[14]

Blicke was brisk and to the point. He ruled out everything but surgery which, he said, could be 'perform'd with safety & good hope of success'. Susan was shocked by his bluntness and felt incapable of following his advice: 'All my ideas are absorb'd in Surgeons, Knives, & wounds, & suffering. God give me the courage to bear my fate.' In a further consultation at the beginning of April Blicke confirmed that she must either have her breast 'cut' or expect the swelling, which he was sure was a cancer, to get worse — and with it the pain, which would be much greater than that of any operation. Blicke told her the operation would be 'without difficulty' – 'that is to say, without difficulty to him,' Susan wryly commented. 'But for me!...' With all hopes of a painless cure dashed, and condemned to a 'dreadful operation', she wrote, 'I hate Mr B (certainly unjustly) for his opinion, but I like him for his decision, clearness, & steadiness — it gives confidence.'

Yet her customary resolve – '*oaklike*', as Lady Sarah had called it — for

---

[14] Blicke would become Master of the Royal College of Surgeons in 1803, when he was also knighted. Despite his eminence, his *ODNB* entry is dismissive about his only published work and cites his apprentice John Abernathy's biographer: 'The tone in which [Abernathy] usually spoke of Sir Charles's practice did not convey a very favourable idea of the nature of the impression which it had left on him. In relating a case he would say: "Sir Charles was at his house in the country, where he was always on the look-out for patients."'

once failed her. She felt little pain from the disease and feared much from the operation. Her brother Ilchester did all he could to support her, though he would not advise her on what course of action to take: 'yet I see he leans to the operation.' But Stephen Digby, to whom she also looked for guidance, would not discuss the subject at all, 'says he cannot bear details — his own misfortunes, & his bad spirits prevent him from being of any use to me…' Her thirty-fifth wedding anniversary on 7 April was a miserable day both for her and O'Brien, who suffered along with her.

In despair, Susan made one last attempt to postpone the day of reckoning. She wrote to Blicke, distancing herself as far as she could by referring to herself, as well as addressing him, in the third person:

> Lady Susan O'Brien's compliments to Mr Blicke, she finds herself so well & so easy that she cannot persuade herself of the necessity of immediately deciding to undergo the operation he recommends — in the first instance & without making some trials of a milder nature - & therefore begs he will tell her what he wd advise her to do, supposing her absolutely determined against it.

Had she stopped there, she might have stood a chance. But she went on (still speaking of herself in the third person): 'She does not say this is absolutely the case, but Mr B must certainly feel how hard a thing it is for any woman without suffering pain, & in all other respects in perfect health & spirits, to determine on such a measure while any possibility remains of escaping it.'

Blicke was unmoved by Susan's appeal. He repeated what he had already told her, 'that the Dread of temporary Pain may in future subject you to a Degree of continual Pain beyond what any Operation could inflict upon you', and sternly reminded her that she had not only herself to consider but all her loving family and friends, especially her husband. He did not wish to rush her into making a final decision – 'your mind left to itself will prove an impartial Judge' – but assured her of his best services if she should decide to go ahead with the operation.

Susan resolved to go ahead — and without further delay. She saw Blicke again on Friday 19 April, when he told her that the swelling was, if anything, more pronounced and no time should be lost. The operation was fixed for the following Monday. Susan fought back tears as she went into the details of her situation and the preparation that would be necessary. It was, she wrote, 'like ordering one's own funeral'.

On the Sunday she went for a walk in Richmond Park with her sister Harriot, who calmed her fears over what might happen to O'Brien if she were to die on the operating table, saying how much the family loved and esteemed

5 A Dreadful Malady

him — that 'they look'd on him as one of themselves' – and promising to give him 'every sort of attention & assistance'. Thus reassured, she slept soundly that night and woke up to a fine morning. She wrote, 'I am sure I feel exactly like a person preparing for execution — perfectly free from pain, with a sort of hardened irritated feel, not to be describ'd. Providence will I hope support me thro this day — for much is to be done, & much to be bourne…'

※

Those were the last words Susan wrote in her journal for nearly ten days. She couldn't hold a pen again until 1 May, when she recorded that though the operation had been performed 'with the greatest skill, humanity, & tenderness' by Mr Blicke her suffering was 'very great & very long'. The first shock was that she was to be blindfolded before entering the room where the operation was to take place:

> [A]s I had no idea that after the resolution I had brought my mind to adopt, it should be suppos'd I cou'd be frightened at the sight of the instruments, & apparatus necessary; & as I had a fix'd determination rather to die than scream & lament, or make any resistance, or even that they should see a tear of mine, I combated it as long as I could.

It was only when Blicke had insisted it was for his sake – 'he could not answer for doing his duty, if he was to see the countenance, & the looks of his patient in such a situation' – that Susan submitted to being blindfolded by Sir Walter Farquhar and Adair Hawkins, who therefore led her 'blinded… to my Execution'.

In Paris twelve and a half years later, Napoleon's celebrated military surgeon, Dominique-Jean Larrey, performed a mastectomy on Madame D'Arblay — better known as the novelist Fanny Burney. Burney was given a wine cordial, probably laced with laudanum, the nearest thing to an anaesthetic then available. If it was intended to stupefy her, it doesn't seem to have worked. She, too, had her face covered, but with a semi-transparent cambric handkerchief. 'Bright through the cambric,' Burney wrote in an extraordinary letter to her sister Esther (the style of which her biographer Claire Harman describes as 'an odd mixture of reportage and melodrama'), 'I saw the glitter of polished steel — I closed my eyes. I would not trust to convulsive fear the sight of the terrible incision.'

In Burney's case at least, there was clearly no intention of preventing the patient from seeing what was happening to her, only of making her as invisible as possible to the doctors — a necessary distancing process if (as Blicke told Susan) they were to do their duty.

Burney's operation lasted nearly twenty minutes and beforehand she had been advised not to resist the urge to cry out. And – 'when the dreadful steel was plunged into the breast — cutting through veins — arteries — flesh — nerves' – she found she 'needed no injunctions not to restrain my cries'. She started 'a scream that lasted unintermittently during the whole time of the incision – & I almost marvel that it rings not in my Ears still! so excruciating was the agony'. But through her screams she was able to take in all that was happening to her:

> When the wound was made, & the instrument was withdrawn, the pain seemed undiminished, for the air that suddenly rushed into those delicate parts felt like a mass of minute but sharp & forked poniards, that were tearing the edges of the wound — but when I again felt the instrument — describing a curve — cutting against the grain, if I may say so, while the flesh resisted in a manner so forcible as to oppose & tire the hand of the operator, who was forced to change from the right to the left — then, indeed, I thought I must have expired. I attempted no more to open my Eyes, – they felt as if hermettically shut, & so firmly closed, that the Eyelids seemed indented into the Cheeks. The instrument this second time withdrawn, I concluded the operation over —

But no, far from it, this chilling account goes on for quite a while yet, describing the 'utterly speechless torture' in detail, the 'rackling' of the surgeon's knife against the breast bone as he scraped away diseased matter, and the way she could actually feel another doctor's finger, pointing out yet more to be removed, though he did not so much as touch her, 'so indescribably sensitive was the spot' – and the further agonising scraping that followed the imperious finger…

In her journal, Susan spares us the gory details that the novelist in Burney finds irresistible, and concentrates entirely on her state of mind during the ordeal which she likens to an execution:

> A kind of self confidence, an exaltation in doing what you ought, what your friends approve, & respect you for doing well — a haughty indescribable indifference about life or death, & a determination of going thro' any part well that you have undertaken. These were the sentiments that supported me thro'

this great effort, & I think the lessons of NA [North America] have not been quite lost on me.

For all her preliminary fears and procrastinations, her courage did not fail her in the event.

Buoyed up by this, and by the 'great satisfaction it has given my dear Mr OB & the extreme kindness of my Family', Susan soon regained her strength. 'Little used as I have been to the soothing & tender attentions of near relations,' she wrote, 'my Sister's care & affectionate behaviour has given me a greater degree of pleasure than I can express.' Harriot and her brother had taken care of the financial side, too, Lord Ilchester undertaking to pay all expenses, and Col. Digby had welcomed the O'Briens into his home at Richmond Park for several months.[15]

By the time Susan went to stay with him at Richmond, Stephen Digby was once again a widower, having lost his second wife just four years into the

---

[15] Stephen Digby provides a further link with Fanny Burney. He met Burney after the death of his wife, Susan's sister Lucy, who had been a contemporary of Fanny's at Mrs Shields's boarding school in Bath and had been particularly kind and protective to her after Fanny's mother died. At the time of their meeting he was the Queen's vice-chamberlain, and he befriended Fanny during her five-year service – or servitude – as second keeper of the robes to the Queen. Despite what her biographer describes as his 'gouty foot, ruined teeth and taste for melancholic literature', he was not unattractive to women. He was in the habit of visiting her room and 'sitting reading Mark Akenside's poetry to Fanny while she got on with her endless needlework, like an old married couple'. According to Harman, Fanny was 'realistic enough to see that Digby's "high family" and his first wife's "still higher connections" made her an unlikely candidate for second wife'. But she was hurt when he dropped her in favour of a maid of honour, 'the young, lovely and rich Charlotte Gunning', and still more so when, after his second marriage in 1790, he avoided her 'like the plague' while still expecting her to mix socially with his wife (Claire Harman, *Fanny Burney*, pp. 214-221).

Caroline Fox (elder sister of the 3rd Lord Holland) would later write: '"Fairly" is an unlikely *nom de guerre* for Miss Burney to have chosen for Mr Digby, who behaved so unfairly to her.' Stephen was 'much cried up by a certain set', but when Caroline – a very astute young woman (and the object of Jeremy Bentham's unrequited love) – met him, she 'judged him to be something of a humbug – and so exceedingly refined & sentimental':

> He married his first cousin Ly Lucy Strangways to whom *dit on* he was the tenderest & [most] faithful of husbands. Nevertheless he had a platonic attachment during her life to Miss Gunning, a maid of honour as refined & sentimental as himself & whom he afterwards married – I think after his acquaintance with Miss Burney solely out of a point of honour – the dupe of his own selfish reserve in concealing an engagement which, had he frankly acknowledged at the outset, their friendship & intimacy which proved such a delightful relief to the dullness of their court attendance, might have continued through life & added rather than endangered… their Domestic Life (Caroline Fox, undated note, Add MSS 51356).

marriage. Whatever his failings, Susan was deeply grateful to him for inviting her to Richmond Park and thus helping her make up her mind to go to London, with 'all the good consequences that journey has had'. And his death the following year was a grievous loss to her: 'He was the person in the Family that I felt more as *friend* than almost any other person. I could talk to him of my affairs, & could open my heart to him on many subjects without being immediately suppos'd to want something — which sentiment I see so constantly uppermost with some others — his advice was always sensible, friendly & practicable...'

Many other friends, including Harry Fox (younger brother of Ste and Charles) and his niece Caroline Fox, had pleased Susan by taking the trouble to visit her – 'but no CF... too indifferent, tho several times in town, to enquire what has become of me.' Charles Fox did write to O'Brien from St Anne's Hill near Chertsey in Surrey (where he was living with Elizabeth Armitstead, the mistress he had secretly married in 1795) on 23 May, saying he had become so unused to seeing people that he had only just heard about Susan's operation. Of course he'd known such an event had been on the cards, but — in a way of keeping unpleasant things at a distance that was characteristic of Charles — had 'hoped that *no news* was good news'. He went on: 'pray let me know how she is and remember me kindly to her, and assure her that nothing can give me more satisfaction than to hear that the Remedy is as complete as it must have been trying to you both.'

In contrast to Charles Fox's correct but cool letter, Lady Sarah (whom Susan had kept in ignorance of her impending operation) responded to the news in her usual fulsome manner. Writing from Dublin, she exclaimed:

> How shall I find words, my beloved friend, to express to you the shock I received when... I learned that you had put into secret practice that exalted magnanimity of soul, which from your infancy has been your marked character!
>
> The surprise brought suddenly before my eyes your sufferings, & I almost hated myself for not having felt all the anxious misery a friend *should* endure in such a case... My dearest Ly Susan, *you* are one of the few living patterns of firmness one ought to set before the eyes of one's children, as the height to which one may exalt courage, patience...

It wasn't until the end of May that the surgeon Blicke — in Susan's words, 'as well as one of the most skillfull, a very humane & feeling man' – expressed himself satisfied with his patient's recovery from her wounds and took his leave. Susan was almost afraid to let him go, though she was pleased to think the whole business was over at last. As yet she hardly dared hope the 'dreadful malady' would not recur.

In mid-June, after an absence of six months, the O'Briens were back at Stinsford, where their neighbours at Kingston, the Pitts, and their many other local friends were as delighted to see them as they were to be there.

One morning in early August Susan had an unexpected visit from Adair Hawkins: 'the sight of him gave such a revulsion to my whole frame that I hardly got the better of it the whole day. What a concatenation of dreadful images did he renew — every transaction of the 22nd April were in an instant as if present. This was certainly an effect of surprise... I was however very glad to see him, & feel the safer for his being near me.'

For Susan was suffering from post-operative depression. After the euphoria of surviving such a climactic event, she sank into a slough of despond. 'I feel very irritable,' she confessed, '& have been very much irritated. It must I think be a difference in health that makes such a difference in the manner that objects of even a trifling nature affect me. At any former time, what has now vex'd me so as to be quite ill, would not have...' On second thoughts, was it not simply the fear of a recurrence of her illness that was getting her down? Mr Blicke did say, in a letter he wrote to O'Brien in October, thanking him for the present of a brace of partridges: 'Lady Susan may be liable to some little variation in her side in consequence of her late sufferings and the uncommon bad state of the weather.' But he hoped she would continue to feel the benefits of the operation and enjoy 'those comforts which she so much merits by her Resignation and Virtues'.

6
PANDORA'S BOX

So long as her own survival had been at stake Susan's habitual anxieties over O'Brien's mental and bodily state, his prospects of finding employment, their finances and chances of remaining at Stinsford, had been in abeyance. Now that she had regained her health, these concerns once again came to the fore. She took advantage of being so much in favour with their Dorset friends to press Morton Pitt and other influential (and mostly Tory) neighbours to do what her own family — and Charles James Fox, in particular — had signally failed to do: to come up with a suitable post for William O'Brien. Previously, Pitt had held back out of delicacy, feeling that Susan's prominent Whig family might resent such interference; but once he learned how matters truly stood with them, no one could have been more zealous in promoting their interests than he was.

For the first few months of 1800, however, she and O'Brien were content to resume their interrupted domestic routine — Susan busy with her needle and 'Mr OB reading to me in our *old way*'. They passed the time pleasantly in each other's company and felt no need to go anywhere but to neighbouring Kingston, where they were always welcomed by the Pitts. But on 14 May, Susan wrote, 'Pandora's Box open'd & a thousand unknown ills rushed out upon me'.

What occasioned this outburst was O'Brien's appointment as one of three commissioners 'for examining the St Domingo Claims', a post that the assiduous Morton Pitt had obtained for his friend.

In his multi-volume *History of the British Army*, Sir John Fortescue writes, 'The secret of England's impotence for the first six years of the war [with revolutionary France, 1793-1798] may be said to lie in the two fatal words, St Domingo' – now Haiti. The British military expedition to the island, which was undergoing a revolution of its own (for ever connected with the name of Toussaint L'Ouverture), was hideously wasteful of money and soldiers' lives. Yet William Pitt and his war minister Henry Dundas agreed to subsidise an assortment of French *émigrés*, the self-styled 'Proprietors of St Domingo', to raise regiments there to promote a British conquest of the island. In return, these Proprietors had to swear an oath of loyalty to George III. But by the time their chief, aptly named Charmilli, arrived in St Domingo, along with '65 Emigrant officers, all with intimate friends in the British Cabinet, and all expecting salaries and appointments', the British had decided to evacuate the island — which they did on 31 July 1798. The task of the commission to which O'Brien had been appointed was to assess the claims for compensation of this bunch of well-connected Frenchmen and their families.

The post was not permanent, of course; the commission would be disbanded as soon as its work was done. But Morton Pitt expected it to go on for two or three years and had no doubt it would 'lead to something better' — a phrase all too familiar to the O'Briens, following their North American experience. The salary was not yet fixed but was likely to be in the region of £500 to £1,000 per annum — enough surely to raise their spirits.

And yet… and yet, as Susan noted, 'I think we may be made miserable by our *good fortune*. Again I feel the pang of leaving this place, the first abode of all the tranquil joy my Life has been season'd with. Again the painful doubts revive of whether we should resign *all we are sure we enjoy & like*, for additional income which will bring additional expense — a London life with nothing at the year's end. Wou'd this tempt either of us? No, no!'

This time Susan and O'Brien were in complete accord; neither of them wanted to be uprooted from Stinsford. But they could not afford to turn down such an opportunity, or to discourage Morton Pitt's efforts on their behalf.

The best news from Susan's point of view was that O'Brien, who'd had to go to London to meet the secretary of the commission, didn't think they would have to leave Stinsford. An official of the commission wrote confirming that 'however Mr O'Brien's friends may wish to see him in London, they cannot be desirous of wholly withdrawing him from his peacable retreat at Stinsford; & perhaps his health would not admit of a constant residence here' — though he added the usual rider that the post, being temporary, was 'of little value, unless it should lead to something permanent'.

The main difficulty was that the commissioners would not be paid until their work was completed — which would take a minimum of twelve months, and might well (as Pitt had predicted) go on for a further year or two. In the interim they had to come up with the means to find somewhere to live in London — for Susan saw that it was necessary for O'Brien, at least, to be there.

She tried to think of some advantages, but all she could see were the inconveniences: 'It is some thing singular that every thing to us must be so very *uncertain* — uncertain whether we should get any thing — now got — *uncertain* what it will prove — *uncertain* when paid, *uncertain* how paid, *uncertain* in duration, & *uncertain* whether it will force us to leave this country — for me that hate *uncertainty* as much as misfortune, this is a good share of it — but it must be endured.'

She told herself that if it lasted only a year she could put up with it. She wrote to her brother to ask for an advance of £500 to cover their extra expenses, but though he was prepared to enter into a bond with O'Brien, repayable on receipt of his salary, Lord Ilchester had no money of his own to offer. In the end, their good friend and nearest neighbour, Rev. William Floyer — whom Susan's mother had appointed vicar of Stinsford on O'Brien's recommendation in 1784 — lent them the money, and before the month was out O'Brien was back in London, summoned by his office.

Susan resigned herself to following him there. She recalled the misery of leaving Stinsford the year before in preparation for what she'd been convinced would be her funeral – 'this year another sort of business — could I but be sure of returning I should not care, but alas, how many chances are against it!'

Soon after Susan joined him in town, O'Brien received a letter from his brother-in-law inquiring how long he expected his new duties to keep him in London. Lord Ilchester's reason for asking was that the farmer at Stinsford, who had been living with his parents, was getting married and needed a house. If the O'Briens intended to leave Stinsford, his plan was to pull down the house and rebuild a much smaller dwelling for his tenant. Alternatively, if they were planning to return, the house was in such a state of decay and disrepair that the best option would be to dismantle one wing of it and use the materials to build a separate farmhouse. Lord Ilchester added: 'I should be very sorry to hurt Susan's feelings on this or any other subject, but I think it fair & reasonable that she should give way in some things as I should give way in all. Some trees must be cut in the lane & elsewhere — those in the lane are much complained of by the public.'

His letter thoroughly alarmed Susan. She was too attached to the place to 'do what pride & present irritation would dictate' – i.e., pack up and leave. If only O'Brien had taken a lease on the house when her mother had wanted him to do that, 'neither this nor many other disagreeable circumstances could have occur'd'. But he was not interested then. As for her brother, 'He says he will not wound my feelings, but I have been too tenacious — tenacious of what? because I have beg'd him to spare some trees –"*Le bouquet d'arbres qui fait l'ornament du pais*".'

O'Brien replied to Lord Ilchester that he couldn't deny that Susan was shocked and agitated, and that, after quarter of a century of living at Stinsford, it was going to be an emotional wrench to abandon all their friends and connections. Nevertheless, 'at the end of my present labours, I shall look out for a place where to pitch my tent once more.' Carried away with the pathos of the picture he was evoking, he continued: 'The world is all before us, and Providence our guide — that Providence which has been so kind and rais'd us up friends even among strangers…'

It's impossible to say if the recipient of this letter was as moved as the writer clearly was by this vision of a couple of ageing nomads or gypsies pitching their tent on some wind-blasted heath. What is certain is that the O'Briens' friends did everything they could to dissuade them from giving up Stinsford.

William Floyer asked if they could not live comfortably in the south wing, if farmer Nichols occupied the remainder of the house, and delicately suggested he might be able to provide a further £500 towards making any necessary improvements there. The Pitts offered to buy the house and let them live there for the rest of their lives, but Lord Ilchester refused to consider selling — as Susan was sure she would have done in his position, 'unwilling naturally to part with any thing in Dorsetshire'. Her niece Lady Harriot Frampton expressed regret at the thought of their not returning to Stinsford and hoped it wasn't irrevocable. She added: 'From the different conversations on the subject I had with Maria, she then appeared not to have the smallest idea of such a thing in my father's thoughts…'

For the time being the matter remained unresolved, though Lord Ilchester made it clear he was not asking the O'Briens to go; he merely wanted to make whatever alterations were necessary to accommodate the farmer.

Susan, marooned in London, was struck by the double bind she was in, her choice being either to live agreeably but in constant fear of 'pecuniary difficultys', or to live disagreeably but relieved from financial worries: 'such is the world! From one plague to another — *Out of the frying pan into the fire* — Elegant conclusion.'

On 1 January 1801, a gloomy Susan wrote: 'The year & the Century begin this day, & a dark & rainy one it is…' By February the political world was in turmoil. William Pitt resigned after failing to carry a Roman Catholic emancipation bill through parliament in the teeth of George III's opposition, and the King himself suffered another bout of insanity. Susan commented: 'Nothing is more strange than *for us* to think Mr Pitt's resignation is a loss *to us*; yet *he* is the only one that has done any thing for us… I will not however injure those who *ought* to help us, so much as to suppose they wou'd not remember Mr OB if occasions offer'd, but disappointments occasion doubts & suspicions.'

Despite these doubts, when a politically reinvigorated Charles Fox, emerging from his St Anne's Hill lair and taking a lease on a house in town, called on the O'Briens, Susan was delighted to see him. They had not met for ten years and she found him 'grown fat & grey, but looking very well'. This unexpected visit 'renew'd a thousand old & affectionate ideas of childhood & youth in my mind, which nothing but a series of neglect & disappointments cd ever have made me forget, or rather try to forget; but when I see him good natured & pleasant it is impossible not to love him & wish him well.' She wrote to Sarah in Dublin (where Napier was now Controller of army accounts) to say how much at ease she'd felt with him, and Sarah replied that it was exactly the same with her: she and Charles met but once in a decade yet it was always a pleasure to see him. But any hopes that Charles may have entertained of returning to office were dashed when Addington (remembered now, if at all, for Canning's epigram, 'Pitt is to Addington,/ As London is to Paddington') became prime minister.

The previous August, Susan had been surprised to receive an invitation to the theatre from Prince William, the son of her old admirer, the Duke of Gloucester. Afterwards she jotted down their banal conversation, during which the Prince quizzed her over her youthful friendship with his father and Lady Sarah's relationship with his uncle, causing her to remark: 'It is extraordinary how much *they all* know on this subject, & how much they like referring to it. It must have made a *great* impression as all these anecdotes are transmitted from generation to generation.'

Susan was flattered to receive this royal attention — having been rebuffed in an earlier attempt to get back into the King's favour (because of the Queen's disapproval, she was sure), after being told that he never forgot an old friend. But on the Prince's side there may have been more to it than idle curiosity over his father's and uncle's youthful romantic attachments. He was at the time lobbying O'Brien, as a commissioner for the St Domingo claims, on behalf of four French ladies in whose welfare he had taken an interest. In his correspondence with O'Brien during the spring and summer of 1801, the Prince expresses his gratitude for 'the great readiness with which you have had the goodness to forward my wishes thro'out this Business' and says how obliged his protégées will be for 'the very liberal Provision that has been made for them' when they get to hear of it — though his later letters suggest that this was far from the case and these French ladies were all for screwing every penny they could get out of the Treasury.

At least the commissioners were now being paid. They received an annual salary of £500, which was just as well since the business of the commission showed no sign of winding up. With that in mind, Susan agreed to let Stinsford House on a short lease to a General Garth: 'The idea that it will help to preserve it makes me willing to have him there — tho otherwise it is not quite a pleasant thing.'

※

By the middle of 1802 Lord Ilchester's health was failing. He accompanied Lady Ilchester to Buxton in Derbyshire, where Maria hoped the waters for which it was famous would aid his recovery. When they stopped off in London, Susan found her brother 'very low, & much averse to going.' With reason perhaps, since after a few weeks during which there were almost daily reports of the benefits he was experiencing, he died there.

Though Susan had never had an easy relationship with her brother, whose status as head of the family had made her so dependent on him, she mourned his loss, not just for the sake of his children but for all of them – 'Melbury *again gone*, now forever probably, from me. Its inhabitants if it has any for many years too young to like my society, or I theirs.' She was surprised by how deeply affected she was, and lurched between sorrow over his death – 'fear my poor Brother had every improper treatment by an ignorant Physician… so unwilling to go to Buxton, such *presentiment* that he should never return' – and anxiety over her own and O'Brien's future: 'what will guardians do for Stinsford, when one's own Brother would do so little?'

Guardians — or guardian? Lord Ilchester's failure to update his will after 1782, when his first wife Mary Theresa was still alive, led to a legal wrangle over the guardianship. Mary had then been named guardian along with Stephen Strangways, but her death meant that Col. Strangways would now be the sole guardian. This was particularly hard on Maria as the second wife with three sons of her own, for whom no provision had been made. Susan sympathised with Maria, who had always behaved 'most kindly and properly' to the children of the first marriage and would surely have been appointed joint-guardian but for Lord Ilchester's negligence, but she disapproved of her decision to make it the subject of a legal challenge.

Before the end of 1802, Harry, 3rd Lord Ilchester, and his two younger sisters who were all still minors, had joined Maria in petitioning Chancery against their uncle being made their guardian; and early the following year Susan was perturbed to hear that Lady Ilchester would 'try every court in England over the Guardianship'. She felt there was 'much unjust prejudice against my Brother Strangways' and blamed the lawyer Maria had consulted for encouraging her to take legal action.

The O'Briens reclaimed Stinsford in July 1803, after the expiry of Gen. Garth's lease. Their friends — in particular the Floyers, with whom they dined on the day of their arrival — were delighted to have them back. But privately Susan felt anxious on several counts: 'I think I see such a deadness in OB to every thing here — such difficultys & expense to get comfortably settled that *I too* feel damp'd & desponding - & leaving it again in three months makes the whole plan useless — all owing to the procrastination at the St Domingo board, or rather of emigrants who delay as much as they can.'

Yet within a week Stinsford had worked its magic and she'd recovered her spirits. The weather was good and a fine St Swithin's Day promised more of the same; there were workmen all over the house, putting things in order; farmer Nichols was 'very civil'; she had her horse again, and now a cow as well – 'I may say I have not pass'd so pleasant a week since I left the place 3 years ago.'

When the O'Briens returned to London in the autumn and William picked up the threads of the interminable St Domingo business, Susan reflected on the summer spent at Stinsford. On the plus side there had been the glorious weather, the opportunity to go out and about in her little chaise once more and the kindly intentions of her brother Strangways over repairs to the house there. But these were not enough to offset the negative feelings brought on by the reserve Lady Ilchester had shown towards her both at Melbury and later on a short visit to Abbotsbury, where the conversation had been confined to the 'most indifferent topics'. She had always respected Maria and treated her as a friend, but she sensed that she was '*no favorite*' of hers. Whether she spoke of the repairs they were undertaking at Stinsford, or of the affairs of Harry, 3rd Lord Ilchester, and his younger sisters Charlotte and Louisa, she got no response from Maria. As a result she had gone home feeling 'quite low, vex'd & out of spirits'.

Maria may have got wind of Susan's disapproval of her going to court over the guardianship and resented that — especially after she lost the case. Or perhaps she had found Susan too ready to take advantage of Col. Strangways' generosity with the Ilchester estate money not just over repairs at Stinsford but in putting the family's Burlington Street house at the O'Briens' disposal when they were in London, thus enabling them to give up a house they'd rented in Queen Street.

Still in London at the end of the year, Susan's thoughts were again focused on Stinsford and how O'Brien would feel about living there once he no longer had business in town:

> he has not the same attachment to the country as I have; he has not the amusements & occupations that I find there — reading is the only thing that can be call'd a pleasure to him, & this is not in pursuit of any particular study but as filling agreeably his leisure hours.[16]

She worried that his eyes might fail, and then what would he do in the long evenings? So she was more apprehensive than ever about setting out for Stinsford. If it didn't work out this time, she felt, 'this World is over *with me*; I shall then be ready for the next'.

※

O'Brien was in London again at the beginning of June 1804. He came back to Stinsford on the 12th, pleased with the way things had gone, and in particular with the termination of the St Domingo business — though he was not so happy about the absence of a final bonus payment for services rendered.

In celebration he had splashed out on a picture, which he wanted to hang

---

[16] Susan and O'Brien were both avid readers. Between 1792 and 1814 Susan kept a list of all the books they'd read each year – a list that demonstrates just how eclectic their taste was. Most of the them are long forgotten, of course, but there are one or two familiar ones. Among the twenty-eight titles listed for 1794, for instance, are: *Mémoires du Duc de St-Simon*, Mrs Radcliffe's *Mysteries of Udolpho*, Arthur Young's *Travels in France*, Mrs Piozzi's *Travels*, Dr Burney's *Musical Tour* and Goethe's *Sorrows of [Young] Werther*.

in place of Susan's portrait by Katherine Read. Susan was unhappy on both counts. She thought they could ill afford such luxuries as to be buying paintings; and she regretted the downgrading of her picture, whose 'strange fate' she charted in her journal: 'Admired by every body as well painted & like, yet always given from one to another of those I thought loved me best — from Ly Sarah to C Fox, from him to OB.' And now it was to be moved out of sight.

Soon after this she heard from Lady Sarah herself, who had come over from Ireland with her ailing husband and was staying at Bristol Hot Wells, which was fast overtaking Bath as *the* fashionable spa. Col. Napier's health, Sarah wrote, had made her 'a most miserable person for near three years! Long sufferings have wasted him to an almost attrophy, & here we came to recover it'. She added a PS: 'I am blind in one eye.' And having lost the sight of one eye completely she was in 'daily risk of losing the other, unless I sit in the dark *musing*, which I cannot bear, & *so* I write, I read, I do all sorts of wrong things'.

The O'Briens hastened to visit their friend and, as Susan later wrote to her niece Lady Elizabeth (whom she insisted on calling Eliza, while the rest of the family knew her as Lily), found her 'well in health, but very low & distress'd at Col. Napier's illness, which I think, & so does she, a very dangerous one — bilious to a great degree, & the lungs affected, tho at present not very much — thinking of Devonshire, of going abroad, & all the useless schemes that illness suggests, for those we love — & the children to get on in the World & the greatest part of their income depending on their Father's life'. In her journal she wrote of Napier, 'he seems to me a lost man,' and marvelled at Sarah's good temper and resignation.

The O'Briens called at Redlynch and Discove on their way home. 'I can't say but that it affected my spirits to see those places again,' Susan told Eliza. 'So it would you, to find poor Redlynch, the seat of your former glorys, look so abandon'd & forsaken, the House unfurnish'd & the shrubbery overgrown & ruinous, & tho the time of my glorys is more remote, yet I assure you I cou'd hardly stand it.' It reminded her of Melbury, where *L'Ange Exterminateur*, as she put it in her journal, had also been at work – 'so many people, so many places, so many pleasant days spent there — all gone & hardly a trace left.'

Susan had barely reached Stinsford before she received an SOS from Louisa Napier urging her to come quickly as her father was dying. Susan set out at once, this time alone, but reached Clifton too late to see the Colonel alive. (Though devoted to Sarah, neither of the O'Briens cared much for Napier, William going so far as to suggest that Sarah and the children would fare better without him – 'For disagreeable he was, to most people'.)

Susan wrote to Charles Fox, informing him of Napier's death, and he replied at once, 'My poor Ly Sarah! how my heart bleeds for her!' He gave it as his opinion that for her there was only one possible consolation and that was her children: 'while we think upon what is lost, to think also on what remains'. But for Susan that was part of the problem. Altogether Sarah had nine children — including Louisa, Napier's daughter from his first marriage.[17] How was she going to provide for them now the breadwinner was gone?

Though Susan was pleased to hear from O'Brien while she was in Bristol, the tenor of his letters was troubling. He told her he had nothing to do but pass his evenings with 'my friends in Calves skin by the fireside' and was finding the poet William Cowper a particularly 'delightful companion'. He added that she was not to think him treacherous, for he would enjoy 'reading him all over again with you'. That much was fine; it was the way he signed off that triggered her anxiety: 'adieu, my dearest soul, you are indeed, whatever you may think, *anima mea*. I should be without you a mere carcase. God forbid that ever should be the case — next to dying together the best would be to have you see me laid to rest.' Reading that made Susan glad she had arranged to set out for home the next day, leaving Sarah in the capable hands of her five grown sons.

In his next letter, which reached her at Tetton (near Taunton), where she was staying with her sister Harriot Acland, O'Brien admitted he had been 'very ill indeed with my giddiness & low to a degree not to be endured or even thought of'. Now, he assured her, he was on the mend and, though he was wretched without her, he begged her not to hurry home on his account.

Susan ignored his plea and came straight home. She found him much better than she'd feared, but it wasn't long before his spirits sank again, though he was unable — or unwilling — to say why. Susan believed he was 'too much discomposed at [the prospect of] having the new farmer resident' in one wing at Stinsford, which she thought unlikely to inconvenience him much. But his low spirits in general worried her: 'My cheerfulness can hardly hold out — his used to support mine. It will be a sad change if his should fail.'

The O'Briens spent Christmas 1804 at Melbury. At church there, Susan was disappointed to find the congregation sparser than it had been in her

---

[17] Sarah had herself given birth to nine children. But she had given her daughter Emily Napier to her childless sister Louisa Conolly for adoption. She had hesitated over this but went through with it out of a mixture of generosity towards a much-loved sister and a sense that it would improve Emily's prospects to be brought up in a wealthy household. (See Stella Tillyard, *Aristocrats*, p. 349.)

mother's day, but pleased to see young Harry set a good example by taking communion. Afterwards her cousin and sister-in-law Maria, who had recently been made a Lady of the Bedchamber to Queen Charlotte, showed her some fine presents she'd received from the King and other members of the royal family. Susan comments acidly, 'She is a great favourite at present; altogether every thing appears to me rather surprising but nothing more so after all that I remember, than Ly Ilchester being a court favourite, & Ly Susan *reliqué dans ses terres* by his Majesty George the 3rd. But all is just — prudence & propriety which is known rises & is rewarded, imprudence sinks, all else that is not known don't signify — How should it?'

She looked back over the year with mixed feelings: 'I flatter'd myself our expense would have been less & that the repairs would have been compleated, but they are not begun & the ruinous state of the House admitting rain in every part, has occasion'd much to be spent even to patch it up for the Winter; time however advances just upon us. We shall I hope end our days here, & whether with or without better furniture or repairs, begins to grow indifferent to me.'

Stinsford — always Stinsford. She could put up with lack of comfort, a leaking roof, a fallen garden wall, even lack of money for repairs or improvements; what she could not endure was any loss of faith or pleasure in the place on O'Brien's part. It was equally essential to her that he share her vision of the good life.

7
Trials of a Tax Gatherer

Even before the St Domingo claims commission concluded its business, O'Brien's friends had been working to get him another, permanent post — one that they knew would particularly appeal to Susan.

Typically, Morton Pitt had been the prime mover in lobbying for O'Brien's appointment as Receiver-General of Taxes for the county of Dorset and his fellow Dorset MP, Francis Browne, had also supported O'Brien's candidacy. Susan wrote, 'It is so desirable for us, & so conformable to my wishes that I fear for the usual disappointments they so often have met with.' But for once she need not have worried; the appointment was confirmed by Prime Minister Addington.

Though there was a deputy whose job it was to collect rates and taxes, O'Brien was the person in charge; and the 'deadness' that Susan had seen in him at Stinsford in the summer of 1803, which she had attributed to 'the procrastination at the St Domingo board', may have had more to do with his feeling of helplessness in the face of such a responsibility. There had been letters from the Tax Office demanding attention; meetings with bankers in Dorchester; worries that the deputy, whose name was Boswell, was deliberately keeping him in the dark over details in the accounts — all these had contributed to 'a return of giddyness in his head'. The trouble was, as Susan had informed Eliza, he was ill-equipped to 'examine Rates & Taxes & assessments & *such miseries*'; and she cited a couplet she thought 'was never more justly apply'd – "Business, which of all things I hate,/ Business, the contradiction of my fate."'[18]

O'Brien had no head for figures and was already doubting his ability to deal with the complexities of tax gathering. When James Frampton (Susan's niece Harriot's husband) had told him the kind of tricks his predecessor had got up to – 'he suffer'd the different parish collectors to keep money a great

---

[18] 'Business! the thing which I of all things hate:/ Business! the contradiction of my fate' – Abraham Cowley.

while in their hands, & then told them they got enough by that, & would give them no poundage [commission] – but charg'd it in his own accounts with Government' – he'd only increased O'Brien's sense of helplessness and inadequacy.

Yet for the first time in his married life O'Brien was financially independent of his wife's family. Over breakfast at Stinsford one morning in February 1804 he had told Susan of his plan to take out a life insurance that would provide for her in the future. While she feared that the time for economy was past, she was touched by the kindly way he'd spoken and grateful for his concern. But she was also troubled by what had brought about this conversation — the increasing frequency of his bouts of giddiness. She felt that only those suffering from a complaint really knew the extent of it: 'God forbid his should be dangerous. What should I do then? I am now so tranquil & happy.'

In terms of employment, the O'Briens owed everything to the prime ministers Pitt and Addington. So Addington's resignation in May 1804 and, even more, William Pitt's death a year and a half later mattered to them. Susan wrote of Pitt: '*My Politicks* have always gone with him,' adding, 'but had they not done so, feeling that I owe my present comfortable situation to his relation's influence with *him*… I shall ever feel a grateful respect for his memory.'

Pitt's demise was Fox's opportunity and though Fox's health too was failing, he rallied sufficiently to return to power at the head of the so-called Ministry of All the Talents, an ill-fated coalition of unlikely elements intent on keeping the rump of Pittites out of power and hopeful of securing a lasting peace with France.

Fox's return to power was productive only of discord in Susan's household. Morton Pitt wrote to O'Brien from London, urging him to take advantage of having a friend now in power, but an out-of-sorts O'Brien replied that he would neither write to Fox nor go to town to apply for anything. Susan disapproved of O'Brien's testy response: 'After the many conversations that have passed with Mr Pitt on these subjects he will naturally think there is some *dessous des cartes* that prevents him.' One or other of them should at least send a short congratulatory letter to Charles and as O'Brien wouldn't, she wrote it — at the same time lamenting that they differed '*so much* on the part to be taken in these sort of situations.'

O'Brien was nevertheless persuaded by Pitt and by Mr Martin of the St Domingo board to write to Fox in the hope that he would put pressure on the Chancellor of the Exchequer, Lord Henry Petty, for a final payment of the commissioners for their work on the French émigré claims. He drew up what Susan called 'a very full, clear account of his case & just claim & made a very proper appeal to his friendship for support' but got no answer to his application, making this the third Fox ministry that had produced nothing but frustration and disharmony for the O'Briens.

Yet when Fox died in September 1806, they were both devastated by the news, Susan far more than she'd anticipated – 'so entirely out of his society — so little occasion to be oblig'd for any services to us — so little probability of seeing more of him — Yet this event renews all former affection — it seems to endear & reunite me again to that branch of my Family — every thing hitherto has been all to the other. The National loss will be great at this juncture — every thing so unsettled — but Politicks are not the question — it is a long known & loved friend that we regret tho' the odious set of both men & women who surrounded him have prevented any pleasure or advantage to any but themselves, to whom his good nature has too long been a dupe.'

Charles Fox had loomed large in the O'Briens' lives; they were torn between admiration of his enormous talent and loveable personality and frustration at his failure to do anything for them when it was (or seemed to be) in his power to do so. For the next several weeks they thought of little else. Caroline Fox wrote that when she had told her uncle of a concerned letter she'd had from Susan, he'd replied, 'I know Ly Susan loves me, & is anxious to hear how I am, tho' she does not tease me with continually writing to enquire.' For Susan, Charles's words were like a message from beyond the grave bearing out her conviction that 'real feeling generally leads to the proper way of shewing it'.

Fox, like Pitt, was buried in Westminster Abbey, though unlike Pitt he was not given a state funeral. Yet it was the proud boast of the Foxite press that his private funeral on 10 October attracted quite as many mourners as Pitt's official one had. On that day Susan noted in her journal, 'Sic Transit Gloria Mundi. How it makes one think! Pitt & Fox with such talents, such genious, such rivalship, such animosity, each in a few months laid within a few yards of each other – "*Each in his narrow cell forever laid*".'

On 28 February 1808, the 3rd Earl of Ilchester came of age and the O'Briens were invited to Melbury to join in the celebrations – 'a fine day smiling on dear Harry — the Park was full of people from all the neighbouring villages, great plenty of meat & beer distributed — Evershot volunteers keeping regularity & order — at 3 o'clock a dinner in the saloon & eating room for 300 people; 2 tables the length of the room & one cross one at the top where Lord Ilchester sat, & did the honours very well, in a very pleasing & popular manner.'

Susan was impressed by her nephew, who was fast becoming a firm favourite of hers:

> After the King & other publick toasts he gave his uncle, Col. Strangways who that day finish'd his guardianship. This sort of kind & publick acknowledgement must I'm sure have pleas'd [the colonel] very much, as indeed it did every body present. There were several young men of Lord Ilchesters acquaintance in the House as well as almost all his near relations — 2 Aunts, 5 Sisters, 3 brothers & Lady Ilchester — every thing was well arranged — each lady sat between a gentleman & a tenant so that all partook of the company & conversation suitable to the day — the evening was turbulent, but altogether considering the number & variety of persons present & the abundance of *victuals & drinks*, every thing was conducted with great propriety & good humour, & the day began & ended as well as possible.'

Susan's strong sense of tradition and *noblesse oblige* — and of her place in the world (despite her unsuitable marriage) – was more than satisfied by this event.

Great though her enjoyment of the occasion was, she and O'Brien were both feeling their age. On an earlier visit to Melbury, Susan had grumbled that it was always so full of people (probably meaning Lady Ilchester's many Digby relations) that 'there cannot be room for another & of course the young & gay must come before *Darby & Joan*'. And during the summer of 1808 O'Brien was ill for some weeks with giddiness, which came to a climax on 16 July, just before dinner, when he experienced 'such a rushing in his head that he thought it was apoplectic'. On this occasion the doctor's remedies – 'leeches, cupping glasses & a Blister' – seem to have worked. But these recurring bouts of giddiness increased Susan's anxiety about his health.

After Harry's coming of age, which put an end to the disputed guardianship, relations between Susan and the dowager Lady Ilchester greatly improved ('dowager' makes her sound old when, as Susan's younger brother's much younger second wife, Maria was of course many years Susan's junior). At Melbury at the beginning of January 1809 Susan found her brother's widow more forthcoming than before. 'Every day,' she wrote, 'increases… my esteem for Lady Ilchester who has display'd on many late & trying occasions, the best principles & the greatest affection for the Family — her behaviour to me is more kind than it used to be, tho I never can persuade myself that she ever lik'd *me* — but one must not be angry because *one* is not liked.'

Certainly Lady Ilchester's position in the royal household had enhanced the marital prospects of her youngest step-daughters. This was evident in Lady Louisa's engagement to Lord Henry Petty, the future Marquess of Lansdowne — a match that was welcomed by Susan and her sister Harriot Acland (who were at Harriot's house when they learned of it) despite Lord Henry's failure to remunerate O'Brien and the other St Domingo commissioners when he was Chancellor during the brief Ministry of All the Talents.

As Receiver-General of Taxes for the county of Dorset, O'Brien was materially better off than he had ever been. But his continuing suspicions that his deputy Boswell deliberately kept him in the dark over critical aspects of the business undermined his health and spirits. Susan's journal entries over two years bear witness both to his anxiety and to her impatience with it:

> *6 January 1807.* Mr OB puzzled & confused with his accounts & full of suspicion which not being at all conversant in that sort of business always inclines him too much to be.
>
> *16 January.* O wrote an apology to Bos[well] which will probably satisfy him but these frequent suspicions of some design to wrong him, destroy all real confidence in a deputy, a steward or even a servant.
>
> *3 May 1808.* … O much more cheerful & comfortable than he was — I flatter myself his own reflexions have shewn him how much mistaken he has been.
>
> *15 May.* … 3 letters from London. I think OB was pleas'd with them, & that his prejudice is wearing off. How can it continue? How could it ever arise?

In July 1809, her niece Harriot Frampton told Susan her mother-in-law had been hearing a number of complaints against Boswell. He was accused of stopping payment of commission to tax collectors in many parishes, though he was charging for it in his own accounts (just as O'Brien's predecessor was alleged to have done). One district had declared it would have no more to do with him and would only pay taxes directly to Mr O'Brien. James Frampton urged O'Brien to accompany Boswell on his next round of tax-collection in the autumn, so that he might see for himself what was going on. And at the beginning of October, O'Brien was, as Susan put it, 'thinking & preparing for *his journey*, not an agreeable one, I'm afraid.'

He set out with Boswell on the 9th to collect taxes and to see what complaints, if any, were made about his deputy. But there was not so much as a murmur until the very last day in Dorchester, when 'all sorts of attacks & accusations were made by 2 of the commissioners, Meech & Gould, & very violent & very improper language'. Boswell defended himself from 'such sudden & unexpected accusations', as a result of which another meeting and a further investigation were proposed.

But it was not just a question of Boswell's probity; word had got around that O'Brien himself was not happy in his work. In November he received what Susan called 'a very *singular sort* of letter' from a Mr Hodges, the gist of which was that he, Hodges, had come to Dorchester in the expectation that he would succeed O'Brien as Receiver-General of Taxes. But — Susan went on – 'finding I suppose he is not likely to succeed him *one way*, he proposes another, & offers him terms if he will resign it'. For her this was an alarming development.

After discussing the matter with Morton Pitt (who was surprised to hear of it), O'Brien declined Hodges's proposal. But Susan wasn't fooled: 'the proposal vexes me & unsettles my Ideas — however it is intended advantageously *for me* I had much rather it had not been made.' Pitt called on Hodges to find out what lay behind his proposal and reported that Hodges 'had been quite unwilling to make it, that it was against his own feelings, but that he was urged on to make it by others, for the sake of his large familly, that he was very sorry he had, & hoped O did not take it ill'. End of story. Or so Susan fervently hoped. But as she wrote, 'it puts new thoughts in people's heads.'

O'Brien stuck it out for a further two years. But on 3 August 1811 he received a letter from Morton Pitt which seemed to preoccupy him; and Susan's suspicions were aroused. She feared he 'was thinking about Mr Hodges old proposal of [OB's] giving up his office to him, or making some change, which I had always hated the thought of'. She knew how unhappy O'Brien was as receiver-general, however lucrative the post might be. On 12 November the year before, she had noted in her journal, 'Mr O uneasy about Boswells books — Pattison [the banker] not quite satisfied with his method; all this frets Mr O, I think without reason…' But since then she had been lulled into thinking that all would be well.

The O'Briens had spent the first three months of 1811 at Penrice on the Gower peninsula in Wales, the home of Susan's niece Lady Mary and her much older husband Thomas Talbot, who was ailing physically and mentally. The change of scenery had done them both good and they'd soon settled into a comfortable routine despite the almost continuously wet weather. As Susan wrote to Eliza: 'We go & settle in Mary's room after breakfast where Mr O'B reads till lunch time, then the children or going out or any thing one has to do, & in the evening as well as we can. Mr T goes to bed early & you know Mr O'B takes out his watch at about Eleven…' But even in Wales O'Brien had been fretting about his work; and as soon as he got home he'd had a long and inconclusive conversation with his deputy.

When Susan asked why Mr Pitt was writing to him, he handed over the letter without a word. Though the subject was what she had feared, she was pleased to see that Pitt by no means encouraged the idea of giving up the receiver-generalship to Mr Hodges. He thought it impracticable, as well as impossible to do without relinquishing a large share of their income. As far as Susan was concerned, 'The letter say'd so much there was little for me to add.'

But O'Brien wanted to talk about it. The following day they went for a walk in the garden and discussed the business at length. He admitted he didn't know who he could trust and confessed his uneasiness at having so much public money pass through his hands at a moment when so many bankers were going broke. Susan conceded there was a risk of that in these difficult times and that cunning and greedy business people seeking to take advantage of every farthing complained about Boswell in such a way as to raise doubts and suspicions in his mind. But she was reluctant to come out with what she really felt, which was that none of this need to have happened if he truly applied his mind to the business.

She hoped their friend Pitt's advice, which chimed so closely with her own opinion, might make a difference. But in this she was disappointed. Ten days after getting Pitt's letter, O'Brien went to see Hodges and drew up a contract — much to her chagrin: 'The whole transaction odious to me. A situation so respectable, so lucrative, so parted with grieves me. All my wishes were gratify'd with it. Now to begin again with calculations, with insurances, annuitys, securitys & all the plagues of former times, it lowers my spirits; *it pinches my heart with pain.*'

The deal was that a portion of the receiver-general's salary would continue to be paid to O'Brien for life and, in the likely event of his predeceasing Susan, to her for the remainder of her life, too. As she saw it, that put them in an invidious position vis-à-vis Hodges: 'To be hamper'd & puzzled with a necessitous man & his keen relations; to receive support from those who are wishing & calculating when our death may relieve what they every day will be grudging us, is terribly repugnant to my feelings. So I think it will be to OB's.'

Staying at Melbury later in August, O'Brien broke the news of his resignation to the young Lord Ilchester and his stepmother Maria, who were not against it. Yet Susan was struggling to come to terms with a decision she so bitterly opposed. She put off telling Eliza about it until late in October, when Eliza was staying with Mary at Penrice. Then she wrote:

> … I must tell you that Mr OB is about resigning his receivership of the county. This I dare say will surprise both you & Mary. It will certainly diminish our income, but I hope we shall have enough to do very well. It has for some time kept Mr OB in such perpetual fears & agitations about Bankers breaking, & having Government money to account for (either living or dead) as well as the same hanging over the head of his securities that it has really made him quite ill, & at last determined him to take this step.

She also told Eliza that she and O'Brien had both been unwell. She'd had a 'violent Rheumatick seizure' that, considering how much her mother had suffered from that complaint in her last years, had lowered her spirits; and O'Brien had grown much lamer than he'd been when they'd visited Penrice earlier in the year: 'he now walks with a stick, cannot attempt to ride, & has just sold his… horse.'

Not even the announcement of Lord Ilchester's engagement to Caroline Murray, daughter of the late George Murray, Bishop of St David's, could raise Susan's spirits. She had not met Harry's intended but Maria had told her that Caroline, 'tho without a fortune wou'd be a fortune in herself'. For Susan it was enough that she should make 'dear Harry as happy as I have [no] doubt he will make her'.

On 6 December O'Brien's successor, Walter Parry Hodges, called on his return from London to say that all the takeover procedures had been accomplished, but that Mr Boswell had lost the deputy's post despite Mr Pitt's advocacy; the banker Pattison had been 'inexorable' in insisting that he himself must manage the whole business.

And what a 'tedious & disagreeable business it has been,' Susan added: 'It commenced contrary to my wishes & ideas of what was desirable for us. We give up a very considerable part of our income [roughly a third], & tho we shall have enough now, & I am provided for in future, yet perhaps Mr OB may be blam'd — altogether I hate the whole thing.'

With O'Brien obviously relieved to be out of office, Susan resolved to try and get over her exasperation with him and 'hope as a true optimist should do, that it is all for the best'. But they were unable to put the matter behind them so long as outstanding business connected with it demanded their attention.

Much of January 1812 was spent haggling over Boswell's accounts. By the end of the month, both of them were overcome with lassitude and Susan wrote: 'I cannot conquer my *ennui*. O is out of spirits tho with no particular reason. I cannot foresee any thing better. Our house will grow less attractive & pleasant, the more we decline company or going out, & grow older & want more enlivening… O seems *unamusable* at least with any thing that is within our reach — 2 rubbers at whist play'd so slow & so sleepy that they do not remove *ennui* — indeed this month & this winter has gone far to remove my long protracted hope of enjoying a placid & cheerfull old age.'

The only immediately cheering prospect was Harry's wedding to Caroline Murray. This took place on 6 February — by which time the dowager Lady Ilchester had vacated Melbury and moved to Abbotsbury. In April the O'Briens went to Melbury for an extended visit – 'quite a family one, which I may say (without too much vanity) is not a dull one'. For the first few days the young Lady Ilchester was too unwell to leave her room, which was frustrating for Harry as well as for her, since this was the first occasion on which they'd received company as a couple. When the new mistress of Melbury finally did come downstairs she made a good impression on Susan:

> … *being at home*, her manner appear'd free, civil & very agreeable; a sort of kindness in it that always pleases; no want of information on any of the subjects that came [up] in conversation, & with many little storys & anecdotes from her residence near Windsor *new to me*, made her conversation lively & entertaining — almost any thing *new* is a treat *to me*, who seldom see any one

that puts *a new idea* into my head, & I am sadly tired of my *old ones*. Susan feared that Caroline might be unhealthy, 'tho those who have known her longer say not'.

On their return home, O'Brien was put out to find a letter querying his accounts. He sent for Boswell, who explained things to their satisfaction. But the damage was done; the letter had aroused O'Brien's latent anxiety and increased Susan's fear that the business would never end. The row between Boswell and the banker Pattison had been rumbling on, with Pattison coming to Stinsford and meeting Mr Pitt there in an attempt to exculpate himself from the accusation of pinching Boswell's clerk from him and O'Brien writing to Pattison to explain accounts which he himself barely understood. With Pattison and Boswell at loggerheads, he hardly knew which way to turn.

Weeks were taken up with trying to sort out the disputed tax accounts. Morton Pitt and the lawyer Charlton Wollaston (half-brother of James Frampton)[19] went through Boswell's books and agreed that the public accounts were accurate, fully backed up by vouchers, and that once they had been passed by the Auditor's Office the handover could be completed. But Boswell had put in a demand for arrears of salary which was excessive, according to Susan's accounts book (O'Brien wouldn't keep one himself); and he had to admit as much when Pitt confronted him over it.

Morton Pitt was doing his utmost to bring the handover of the receivership to a satisfactory conclusion but, while nobody could find anything amiss with Boswell's accounts, the mutual antipathy between him and Pattison meant that the latter would not pay in the balance demanded without a special authority from the Auditor to do so. At Pitt's suggestion O'Brien wrote to London and got such an authority; and though Pattison accepted it, he said he couldn't pay the balance till after his next collection of taxes.

'Thus stands the business,' Susan wrote on New Year's Eve, 'which it is pretty clear won't conclude before the long desir'd Lady Day [25 March], when neither party can hinder its being final... & I hope to hear no more on a subject so disagreeable to me in its intention & in its execution.'

---

[19] Charlton Byam Wollaston's father (also called Charlton) was physician to the Queen's household and a Fellow of the Royal Society. His mother was the only daughter and heir of Samuel Byam, a landowner in Antigua. After the death of Charlton's father, she made a second marriage to James Frampton (Sr) and Charlton became and remained very close to his step-family. Educated at Winchester and Cambridge, he was called to the bar in 1809 and practised on the Western Circuit. He later became Recorder of Dorchester and chair of the quarter-sessions. He lived to the age of 75 and, when he died, he was buried in the Frampton family vault (see Hutchins, *History of Dorset*, vol I, p. 399).

7 Trials of a Tax Gatherer

A pleasant June day in 1813 tempted O'Brien to go out for a walk. Susan went to meet him on his return. This was just as well, as he dropped his stick twice and would have fallen had she not been there to hold him up. After walking 'in a very tottering manner' and attempting to climb two or three steps, he collapsed. Susan summoned help to get him inside and sent for the doctor.

The physician Christopher Cooper, who often dined at Stinsford, brought along his colleague Arden, who didn't.[20] The pair of them took a gloomy view of his condition, fearing it might be of a 'paralitic nature'. But O'Brien made a swift recovery; he was even quite cheerful, though well aware of the nature of his seizure. He called it 'the first summons' and clearly expected others. Susan noted that he was 'perfectly resign'd & hoping for my sake as well as his own not to have a long illness. I can hardly express what my heart feels on these occasions, but he don't seek them, they come quite naturally.'

Morton Pitt and Charlton Wollaston dined at Stinsford on 3 August, but Mrs Pitt was too ill to come, causing Susan to remark, 'No cheerfulness now at any of my neighbours.' The next day, when she herself was feeling rheumaticky and low, she elaborated: 'Mr Floyer wishing himself in a better world, Mrs Pitt talking of death & funerals, Mr of schools & the points of Calvinistical & Evangelical difference, O saying he is fit for nothing & will never go from home again; & today a party of *Parlez vous* as I never desire to see assembled again. How shall I go through with it? I must *civilly* & *gayly* or nobody else will.'

On the 7th she spent all day alone in the garden, thinking about what Mr Pitt had been saying about religious doctrine and finding it surprising that 'any man in his senses can seriously maintain cheerfulness & content to be a sin, & that do what we will we should always be in a state of contrition & fear of God's wrath'. But the Pitts had recently lost their only child, a daughter who had made a good marriage and seemed well set up in life, and that had sadly changed their outlook.

A few days later, when Mrs Pitt called, Susan was appalled to hear her say she would 'rather die than go to the Opera'. She feared that she and

---

[20] Surgeons, or surgeon-apothecaries (as Arden probably was) were then regarded as socially inferior to physicians. The surgeon-apothecary's function was in many ways similar to that of the modern GP.

O'Brien might no longer be considered 'good enough' for Kingston now that Mrs Pitt was limiting her society to 'those call'd *Evangelical* & *saints*'. Only at Melbury, where they spent a week in September, did she feel any pleasure: 'I see my family good & happy. They shew us great kindness. The weather was charming & the place delightful. I was better than before we went, & all things have contributed to make my return cheerful & pleasant.'

Susan's mood generally reflected the state of O'Brien's health. For most of September he was better than for some time past. But his condition rapidly deteriorated. On 5 October he was far from well – 'had an awkwardness in his speech & very great weakness in his hand' and, dining out four days later, was so giddy that he fell and Susan had to take him home. Again he recovered quickly. But these recurrent bouts of illness were wearing her down, too: 'I feel it is only by him that I hold on to this world or to happiness in it, & I see his health so visibly declining that it almost breaks my heart.'

They struggled through a dismal November and December. O'Brien had to move to a ground-floor room, as climbing the stairs had become too arduous for him. Everything conspired to make Susan miserable. Mr Floyer uncharacteristically declined their invitation to Christmas dinner and she was so angry with him, with herself and with everyone else that she stayed away from church – '*wrong*, my action *wrong*, my motive *wrong* — but so it was & I am sorry for it.' Floyer, too, was sorry and later apologised for his unkindness.

In early January 1814 there was a heavy snowfall – 'the trees beautiful & like Canada'. Lady Ilchester gave birth to her first child, a daughter, and the news from France was cheering. Susan heard that as soon as the English had crossed the Pyrenees into France the Basque conscripts had deserted in droves and made their way home, where their families hid them. Some French officers who had been taken prisoner had openly admitted their helplessness when, as the first shots rang out, the young conscripts had thrown away their muskets, fallen flat on their faces and cried out, '*La campagne est fini.*' Yet Susan was far from convinced it was over: 'I can't help thinking that Bonaparte will revive again somehow or other & plague us as usual.'

On 6 April the Stinsford church bells rang all day to celebrate the Allies' entry into Paris. Had it been the next day, the O'Briens might have been forgiven for thinking it was in their honour, since the 7th was their fiftieth wedding anniversary — a landmark that Susan was pleased to record in her journal:

> Few have struggled thro more difficultys; few have met with more affectionate kindness; & very few indeed have so long had so amiable & so agreeable a companion as I still enjoy, & cannot be too thankful for.

Now that O'Brien was at last well enough — and willing — to travel, she was eager to go to London to participate in the celebrations of the victorious Allies. But so many people wanted to see the visiting European royalty and dignitaries that rooms were hard to come by, and it was only when they heard there were some available at the Clarendon Hotel that they finally made up their minds to go.

Charlton Wollaston was one of several people who called on them shortly after their arrival there. He wrote to his half-sister, Mary Frampton: 'I... found them in their former apartment, which is as much out of the way of sights as if they were at Stinsford. He looks better than when I saw him last, and seemed cheerful and pleasant; but Lady Susan had evidently begun to anticipate the probability of not getting to any of the sights and gay things which had been her principal object. The Lansdownes are gone [to Paris], and Lord Ilchester also. Mrs Lionel Damer goes out of town for a fortnight on Monday or Tuesday, so I cannot help fearing they may be disappointed and want society.'

Susan did see Sarah and was saddened to find her 'a good deal alter'd, low & engag'd in business'; O'Brien went for a walk and caught a cold; together they visited Westminster Abbey, where Susan judged Pitt's monument 'handsome but too high' and was almost overcome when she was shown 'where poor dear Charles Fox lies'. Otherwise it was just as Wollaston had predicted, the absence of Lord Ilchester and the Lansdownes, in particular, meant that they left London at the end of three weeks – 'as unpleasant a three weeks as could be,' Susan grumbled.

They arrived at Stinsford on 1 June after a wet journey. O'Brien's cold had turned into a bad cough and that had been another reason for leaving town sooner than they'd intended. Susan was, as she admitted, vexed not to have witnessed 'what will never be seen again — the Emperor of Russia & King of Prussia, & Gen. Blucher, & Hero's of all nations, in London'. Two days later she read in the newspapers about the signing of the peace treaty and, with the Stinsford church bells pealing all day as a reminder, could only think of all she was missing – 'Illuminations, Cossacks, &c, everybody setting out to see some thing but me'. When a number of well-meaning neighbours called the next day, she wrote ungraciously, 'I feel so cross that I hate the sight of them'.

Slowly she settled back into the rhythm of Stinsford life, and O'Brien grew strong enough to go out for a walk and a drive with her. But one day when they were sitting together after dinner he 'fell as if shot, on the floor'. Susan was thoroughly alarmed; she rushed to his assistance and asked him what had happened. All he could say was that 'his head turn'd'. There were no paralytic symptoms and two weeks later he was well enough to accompany Susan to a supper party the local farmers gave for their workers in the servants' hall at Stinsford and 'drink a glass of strong beer with them & to them, which they very heartily returned to us'.[21]

Towards the end of July, Susan's now widowed niece Mary Talbot and her young family paid an unexpected visit and they all had a cheerful time – 'O always pleased & better for Mary's company'. While Mary was staying O'Brien surprised everyone by going into Dorchester to sit on the grand jury and dine with the judges. For some time he had been talking about the possibility of their going to France, now that the war was over, to take advantage of the warmer climate there; but after Mary's visit — and much to Susan's relief — he seemed to forget about that.

Not for long, though. When the Pitts called on 23 September, Mrs Pitt was all for going to France — proposing that they all went together. The plan was to do the journey in stages: first to Guernsey, then to St Malo, from which it was only 150 miles to Tours — a mere nothing. Susan was outraged: how could they suggest such a journey to a man who couldn't even walk upstairs unaided? Her surprise at the Pitts' making such a proposal was matched only by O'Brien's readiness to agree to it. She reckoned she was the only person competent to judge just how unfit he was to undertake such a journey; but if his heart was set upon it and she openly opposed it, he would resent that. The peace with France, however welcome in other respects, seemed likely to create problems for her personally.

---

[21] Seventy years on Thomas Hardy recorded the death of 'old Billy C——- at a great age' and what Billy had said about Lady Susan O'Brien: 'She kept a splendid house – a cellarful of home-brewed strong beer that would a'most knock you down; everybody drank as much as he liked.' As a boy, Billy had assisted the gardener at Stinsford who, he said, 'was drunk every morning before breakfast'. And 'on wet days we used to make a point of working opposite the drawing-room window, that [Lady Susan] might pity us. She would send out and tell us to go indoors, and not expose ourselves to the weather so reckless' (see Florence Hardy, *The Early Life of Thomas Hardy 1840-1891*, pp.213-214).

The Pitts came round again after church on the following Sunday, still harping on the French project. Mrs Pitt now thought it might be better to spend the winter in Brighton and go to France in the spring. Which suited Susan, as any postponement increased the likelihood of it never happening. But O'Brien was not prepared to let it go so easily. When Mr Pitt called on his own a week later, he reiterated that he and Mrs Pitt wanted to put off going to France till the spring. But Susan could see no reason for O'Brien to go there at all unless it were to spare him the rigours of an English winter. She wondered how long he thought it would be necessary to remain at Tours if, as she expected, he found no benefit in being there; and if he did feel better, she asked him, were they never to come back? To which he replied, 'No great matter if we don't.'

Susan could not let that pass; with Mr Pitt as witness, she told him flatly that though she would not refuse to go to France or do her duty as far as she could, she would never agree to leave home with no prospect of returning. Just then they received a letter from her niece Lady Louisa Lansdowne in Paris, telling them how unpopular the English now were in France and how disagreeable that was — which, as Susan gratefully remarked, was 'quite *apropos*'.

Any doubt that she had been right to resist O'Brien's desire to go to France was removed when he was suddenly taken very ill in the small hours on the morning of 21 October 'with a shortness of breath so painful as almost amounted to suffocation'. This was a new symptom. Susan was unimpressed with the doctors' explanation that it 'proceeded from the bowels being loaded' and thought it more likely to have other, more dangerous causes. O'Brien, who continued to suffer from these attacks of shortness of breath, called them asthma, and Susan was just as sceptical about that.

Though she was powerless to relieve O'Brien's symptoms, her name was apparently enough to cure others. Mr Floyer called to tell her that Farmer Russell's wife had only consented to get into the warm bath that had saved her life when she was told that 'My Lady recommended it'. My Lady was flattered – 'What nonsensical heads these poor people have! I am glad *My Lady* had such a good effect.'

***

At the beginning of 1815, Susan noted that O'Brien was 'still so ill as to deprive him & me of all cheerfulness & society'. On 14 January a party from

Abbotsbury consisting of Maria, dowager Lady Ilchester, Susan's nieces Eliza and Charlotte and her great-nephew Henry (Fox) Talbot came to visit.[22] Eliza was currently out of favour with Susan for 'not writing, & total neglect' but showed enough penitence *'à sa manière'* to mollify her exacting aunt.

A week later various neighbours came to dine, but O'Brien, who'd had a bad night and was suffering from a cough, found no pleasure in anything. Susan, herself exhausted and ill, did all she could to entertain their guests, questioning a Mrs Martin about her grandfather Captain Fry, whom Susan remembered her father talking about: 'She said he had brought home from the South Sea the famous Alexander Selkirk (the model of R Crusoe) – that he liv'd & dyed at Bruton, was very shrunken, & generally express'd himself by half words, pronouncing only the 1st syllable where there were two.'

Deprived of more stimulating company, Susan eagerly latched on to this curious but trifling anecdote. The following entries in her journal are more typical of this time:

> *23rd [Jan 1815].* a letter from Mr Floyer — our groom got the measles.
>
> *28th.* O very ill & low — bad weather — could not get out in the air.
>
> *31st.* call'd on that odd woman Mrs Henning — had a deal of discourse about Quakers, & different sects — Quakers a very harmless one but very nonsensical.

In February Susan took O'Brien to Bath in the hope he would benefit from the waters or simply from a change of scenery. But far from improving he seemed to get weaker by the day and they were glad to come away after less than a fortnight there. In March came news of Bonaparte's escape from Elba and rapturous reception by the French people, which Susan thought 'most wonderfull' considering how he had 'tyranniz'd so cruelly over them'. Mr Pitt, returning from London, didn't think Bonaparte could possibly succeed and almost welcomed his escape, since it had taken people's minds off the unpopular Corn Bill (which, by taxing imported wheat to protect farmers, pushed up the price of bread). In that case, Susan thought, it was 'the first good he has ever done us' – though she might have added that he had done her personally a favour by rendering a journey to France with the Pitts in the spring unthinkable.

The news from France got worse, culminating in Louis XVIII's ignominious flight from Paris. Susan bemoaned the fact that it would once again be 'all war & misery & discontent & taxes'. To add to her irritation she

---

22 William Henry Fox Talbot, the future polymath and pioneer of photography

got a letter from Eliza – 'all rhapsody & nonsense about Paris — the happiness of Paris… lamenting her own disappointment at not going to that Paradise'. There was not a word in it, Susan wrote, 'that I care a pin to hear.'

Good Friday brought nothing good to Stinsford, only bad weather and more bad news from France, with Napoleon entering Paris in triumph. On 28 March Susan spent the whole day reading to O'Brien, first the newspapers, then Sir Walter Scott's novel *Waverley*. She didn't think she could have read aloud for so long, especially as she wasn't enjoying the novel as much as her sister Harriot had; and she didn't think O'Brien liked it at all. But these days reading was almost the only thing she could do to amuse him.

In April, with the coming of spring, he did perk up a bit. He'd been prescribed ass's milk and that seemed to be doing him good. But as soon as Susan's worries about him went into abeyance, her own health problems — swollen feet, rheumatism, pains in her side — loomed larger. Since his complaints were so much more momentous, hers generally went unnoticed. She thought that was just as well; she had 'so little to animate or make life agreeable that if I was not necessary & useful *to him*, its conclusion would be no great misfortune'.

For a while O'Brien's spirits held up well. On one long warm evening they drove out to Yellowham Wood with Mrs Floyer, hoping to hear nightingales: 'None sang — How often have I gone out with my Mother on the same pursuit — too old for most amusements, we seek those natural ones that time does not preclude.' But her attempts to get O'Brien to share her delight in nature generally and her garden in particular, now that it was in full bloom, were unavailing. She found it impossible 'to say how great a damp it is to ones spirits when those we love enjoy nothing that we do'.

First thing in the morning of 23 June a notice came from Dorchester proclaiming 'a compleat Victory over Boney' at Waterloo. But for Susan any sense of triumph was immediately eclipsed when she read in the *Gazette* that her youngest brother Charles's second son Tom Fox-Strangways had been severely wounded.[23] Fortunately, Tom's wound turned out to be less severe

---

[23] As a lieutenant in the Royal Horse Artillery, Tom F-S had been in the thick of the action in La Haye Sainte when he was hit by cannon fire. It was several days before he could be evacuated to Brussels to have the ball extracted. On attachment to the Swedish force in the Allied army at Leipzig nearly two years earlier, he had so distinguished himself when he took over from his fallen CO, Col. Bogue, that the Crown Prince of Sweden and the Emperor of Russia, Alexander I vied with each other to be the first to decorate him for bravery on the spot. Four decades later, with the acting rank of brigadier-general, he served on Lord Raglan's staff in the Crimean War, where he was shot through the leg at the battle of Inkerman and died of his wounds. (See *Mary Frampton*, pp. 164-66, footnote.)

than had at first been feared; and Susan could again consider the larger picture. After all the excitement occasioned by the Allied entry into Paris fifteen months earlier, this time round there was a sense of anti-climax.

In mid-July Susan heard that Harriot Acland was ill and, since O'Brien was reasonably well, set off at once for Tetton House, determined not to allow her only surviving sister to die without seeing her, however briefly. Harriot had visited Stinsford that Easter and Susan had felt uneasy about her then. Now she found her in a far worse state than she had imagined.

She did what she could for her, though 'an hours walk in her pretty garden & amidst her favorite flowers only helps to lower my spirits, which I wish so much to keep up that at least while I am here I may be of some small use to so suffering & so dear a sister…' Harriot had outlived all of her immediate family, her husband (by more than forty years) and all three of her children, and in her last years she had become something of a recluse. As the last surviving daughters of the 1st Lord Ilchester, she and Susan had grown very close, their youthful quarrel long forgotten.

It broke Susan's heart to leave Harriot in such a forlorn state — but O'Brien was growing fretful and impatient for her return. She had hardly got home before she received a letter from Harriot's doctor, holding out no hope. Had she realised just how close to death Harriot had been she would not have left her when she did. All she could do now was alert her brother Col. Strangways to the imminence of his favourite sister's death.

The funeral took place at the Acland family home of Killerton in Devon on 28 July. Susan was unable to go; instead she sat at home and read the funeral service in the Prayer Book – 'so fine, so sublime, so delightful to those who expect everlasting rewards for temporary sufferings'. Such a contrast, too, to the religious book that the well-meaning Mrs Pitt brought her the next day, which failed to give her the slightest comfort. She loathed the tone of these evangelical books. She thought they did more harm than good: 'they frighten & disgust young minds — who that feels innocent & means well can seriously say they are the greatest sinners — that all their affections & pleasures are offensive to God & denials of the Saviour. Talking of this very book my poor sister said, "Why can't they let one alone, to believe the things we were taught in our youth, & do all the good we can to merit the favor of God?"'

Col. Strangways went to Harriot's funeral and called at Stinsford on his way home. He'd been pleased with the warm reception the family had received from Sir Thomas Acland, but was badly missing his closest friend – 'always judging & acting rightly' – and conscious of how few of them were left. Susan was now the only sister, a thought that gave her no pleasure: 'Older than any, [I] ought to have gone first, but have such good health that I may be (as an Old Woman once said) left at last like a Pollard in the Copse.'

In the first week of August all the news was of Bonaparte's coming to England on board HMS *Bellerophon*. Susan could understand that people were curious to see him but 'after all the injurys he has done us individually & as a nation, after all his ravages & crueltys, that he should become an object of compassion, & respect, is perfectly incomprehensible — Admirals & Captains complimenting him with Naval honors, country people offering him flowers &c, & writers exerting themselves to praise & admire him & pity his case — nay, even blame *us* for cruelty.' She'd always feared 'the mischief his coming would do, if he landed'.[24] So she wished him a speedy departure to his 'second Island', where she hoped he would be better guarded than in his 'first Little Empire'.

But she had little time to reflect on such matters. On the 8th she noted that O'Brien had had a bad night, in which he'd suffered a great deal. She spent all that day alone, sitting under a favourite tree and trying to read Mrs Pitt's book, which was altogether too enthusiastic for her taste. On the 14th she replied to a letter from Eliza: 'I can tell you how Mr O'B passes his time, but not how he amuses himself, for alas! I can't find that any thing does amuse him. He is so weak that he goes early to bed, & candle light don't do for him to read...' On the 30th all she managed to write in her journal was, 'much alarm'd — every appearance worse', and the next day, 'Cooper & Arden here early — could not speak to them. Cooper again in the evening — told me he could give me no hope — beg'd me to be prepared for the worst. I told him I was for every thing. I assum'd all the fortitude I could muster — but it was a death stroke indeed.'

---

[24] Napoleon was not permitted to land, of course, though his ship attracted shoals of little boats both in Torbay and at Plymouth, where it was anchored while the government arranged for his removal to distant St Helena. (For a detailed account of his twenty-four days on board the *Bellerophon*, see David Cordingly, *Billy Ruffian*, pp. 228-279.)

For the next eleven days Susan was too distraught to write a word. She kept a note of '*His* list of the last company *he* invited to dinner 19 August 1815', six guests including Dr Cooper, Rev Floyer, the banker Pattison and Miss Wightwick.[25] Below this list she had transcribed the little verse that she, egged on by Lady Sarah (with whom she had been staying), had sent to the glamorous young actor fifty-three years earlier — the one that had alerted O'Brien to the nature of her interest in him:

> In my silence see the Lover,
> True Love is by silence known;
> In my Eyes you'll best discover
> All the power of your own.

---

[25] Miss Wightwick, the daughter of an old family friend or retainer, had stayed with Susan before when O'Brien had been ill – 'a very comfortable circumstance,' Susan wrote on 9 August 1808, 'being… a person I have known from a child & who I am persuaded has a regard for me' (Ly SO'B's Journal, Add MSS 51359).

PART FOUR:
Joan Alone

The better days of life were ours;
The worst can be but mine:
The sun that cheers, the storm that lowers
Shall never more be thine.

— (Lord Byron, 'And Thou art Dead, as Young and Fair')

'[I] ought to have gone first, but have such good health that I may be (as an Old Woman once said) left at last like a Pollard in the Copse.'

— (Lady Susan O'Brien, *Journal*, 31 July 1815)

8
THE ABSENT ONE

William O'Brien breathed his last at precisely 1 a.m. on 2 September 1815. For the two previous days he had been unable to speak or take any food or medicine, though he would occasionally seem to swallow a teaspoonful of broth; and for the last several hours he had struggled for breath. But there was no convulsion at the end; he just quietly gave up the ghost. Miss Wightwick, a veteran of deathbed scenes, observed that nothing could have been easier — to which Susan responded, 'Heaven grant it was so.' She was grateful for Miss Wightwick's soothing presence, and for the kindness of all her friends – 'but alas! what friends can make up for the one gone.'

She tried to bear her affliction 'with fortitude', but writing down what had happened was enough to bring on a fresh outburst of grief (and play havoc with her syntax):

> Oh what a heartbreaking sight to see one so dear going so visibly from me & cannot tell me what he suffers, if he wants any thing — some think he knew my voice, when I attempted to feed him — but who can say, perhaps only a sort of instinct when he felt the spoon to attempt to swallow. If he did know my voice, it was the last voice heard. Oh would that he could still hear it.

O'Brien's funeral took place on 9 September. For Susan it was like a second death, 'almost as bad as the first'. But she took pride in the fact that everything went according to plan: 'I wish'd it should be here — that [Stinsford] Church should contain our remains — that Floyer should do the last office for his friend, that my dear Nephew & Brothers should attend, that every appearance should shew what every heart felt, regret for so amiable, so pleasing a companion & friend — every servant for so easy & kind a master.'

8 THE ABSENT ONE

The support of her family and friends enabled her to endure the ordeal of O'Brien's burial, and her niece Harriot Frampton stayed on until the 11th, amusing Susan as much as her 'heart would bear amusing'. But when Harriot left to go to Weymouth Susan had a sudden vision of what life without O'Brien would be like – 'I have no occupation — nothing to do — no care for his ease or contentment to occupy my thoughts or employ me — all is gone — *I* am now an object of care to others — How new! I never was so before.'

Susan was a practical soul, both rational and strong-minded, and even in the extremity of her grief she was determined to honour O'Brien in death in the manner she felt he deserved. When Morton Pitt called the next evening, she spoke to him of her wish to *mark the spot* of O'Brien's grave by having his name inscribed, along with the words her heart dictated, 'A Man Amiable & Beloved'. She also told Pitt of her wish to be buried alongside her husband. Plans for a suitable memorial for O'Brien would occupy her for many months to come and involve other sympathetic friends besides Morton Pitt.

She spent several days going through old letters and papers, tearing up those that had been kept only for reference. This was a 'melancholy employment' and she found the letters from O'Brien – 'always anxious for my being well provided for' – particularly distressing to reread. Yet though she appreciated the efforts of friends to distract her, 'silence & solitude fit best with my situation & with my mind'. When Lord and Lady Ilchester called on 18 September, she accepted their invitation to go to Melbury the following week but was very much in two minds over it: she knew the change of scene would be good for her but could hardly bear to be parted from O'Brien — even in his grave.

In her journal she marvelled at her own volatility. On the 19th she wrote: 'Nothing can be more extraordinary to myself than my feelings have been today. I pass'd last night in tears — I could hardly support myself yesterday — this day I feel a Stoical hardness as if nothing could affect me — I can read letters, verses, without a tear. Is my heart harden'd? Am I stupefied? Is memory leaving me? I cannot understand myself. Sure I don't love my dear departed friend less than I did yesterday — what can occasion this difference?' She need not have worried; for her there was no shortening of the process of mourning (or reducing the intensity of her grief).

On the 21st both the Pitts came, and Mrs Pitt gave her 'a book of consolations under misfortunes', which she found 'as good & reasonable as any thing on the subject' but that was as far as it went. She was able to get through the days calmly enough, but her nights were given over to thoughts of the *One*. Bills kept coming in even at this time and Susan feared she would not be able to maintain the size of her 'family' (by which she meant household) as it had been in O'Brien's lifetime, which she regretted — for 'they are good servants'.

When she left for Melbury on the 25th she had been a widow for little over three weeks. She was sorry to leave home, no matter how much everything there affected her — for 'the separation seems greater'. O'Brien was five years older than Susan; had he lived another four weeks he would have been seventy-seven. She tried to take comfort from the thought that he'd lived to a good age and died honoured and respected by family and friends and 'belov'd by servants', but that only brought home to her how much more she, as the survivor of so long a marriage, was to be pitied.

Lord and Lady Ilchester could not have been more solicitous – 'they have hearts, they feel my situation & they know my loss'. She could not ask for more. She found it easier to go to church at Melbury than at Stinsford, where O'Brien's mute presence was still too much for her.

Yet she left Melbury on 9 October and returned to her 'sad destitute house'. In the misery of coming back to an empty home she felt even more her lack of occupation and purpose: 'My life is become a blank — a sort of *dead life*, without the rest of death or the enjoyment of life, a passive life that can be of use to no one, & a charge to myself.' Rev. Floyer came to see her and she went to church the following Sunday, but it was a struggle and she felt ill all day, though she was gratified to be 'so near *him*, so near our long home'.

※

In early November, after much dithering, Susan accepted the Ilchesters' invitation to spend the winter at Melbury. When she arrived the house was full of people and for the first time since O'Brien's death she saw Eliza, who came to her room and 'profess'd great kindness towards me, said if she had not met me here she should have come to Stinsford &c &c'. But after that first night Eliza hadn't said a word 'on any subject that could interest or even amuse me'. Her neglect rankled and Susan observed her with a cold eye: 'still E in her usual way coquetting — that being her stile would not surprise me — tho it is time to leave it off — but it does seem strange that she takes no notice of me more than any common acquaintance she met in the House — but O always told me I was a dupe.'

Her relationship with her eldest niece, who occupied the same position in the 2nd Lord Ilchester's family as Susan had in the 1st Earl's, had always been particularly intense. Eliza was her favourite, but this did not mean she was uncritical — far from it. It was a mark of her own childlessness perhaps that she should treat Eliza more like an errant daughter than a much loved niece. She did not hesitate to find fault with her behaviour and scold her both for things she did and, just as often, for things she omitted to do.

She had disapproved of her first marriage — to William Davenport Talbot — entered too lightly upon, as she (and others) felt; she had disapproved even more strongly of the way she neglected her husband when he was dying; and she had been unenthusiastic when Eliza married again — a successful match with Capt. Charles Feilding — as she disapproved of second marriages on principle. She often accused Eliza of neglecting her and writing letters too infrequently. But when Eliza did write, she was quick to criticise. It must have seemed to Eliza that nothing she said or did would please her exacting aunt.

Although Eliza loved and respected Susan, she was an equally strong character, more than capable of holding her own. After the 2nd Lord Ilchester died, Susan (who was in London at the time) was entrusted by the children's guardian, Stephen Strangways, to deliver a letter Eliza's father had written to his eldest daughter. Susan duly handed it over but Eliza pocketed the letter unopened. This irritated Susan, who told her she wanted her to read it there and then and, if she would, copy it so that it might also be given to her sisters. Eliza's response was cutting; she told Susan to mind her own business; she would deal with it in her own good time. This led to a blazing row between them in which Eliza asked if Susan thought she was going to suppress the letter and Susan replied yes, very likely, if it suited her. For several days after there was a stand-off between the two of them until O'Brien, who could endure it no longer, interceded.

Now brooding in her room — and with no O'Brien to intercede — Susan determined to have it out with Eliza before her niece left Melbury. She got her opportunity on the morning of 27 November, when they found themselves alone in the drawing room. Eliza said she hoped her aunt would write to her often — to which Susan replied, 'I don't know that I shall, for your behaviour since I have been here three weeks has been as if I was a stranger, somebody you had chanced to find in the house, & so perfectly indifferent to you that you have not said one word to me on any thing I could care about, indeed if it was not for my dress you would not remember I was a Widow.'

At this point her pent-up feelings overwhelmed her and she burst into tears. Eliza, surprised and moved by this outburst, protested that she had the greatest regard for her, had thought that she had chosen to be alone and had therefore respected her wish for privacy. She insisted she'd always loved her aunt best, which mollified Susan and made her 'more inclin'd to believe she spoke at least her *present sentiments*'.

Eliza went on to say that she had long known how greatly O'Brien disapproved of her. Susan denied this, saying it was 'not till her behaviour in publick & private fix'd her in his opinion as a decided coquette, a character which he detested, both as unfeeling & mischievous…' But before she could say any more on the subject, the arrival of someone else in the drawing room disturbed their *tête-à-tête*.

That evening a contrite Eliza came to Susan's room and begged her 'not to cast her off'; she couldn't bear that Susan should think her so unfeeling as she had represented her. She seemed to want to continue the morning's conversation but Susan was reluctant to go further into either O'Brien's opinions or her own in her present state of mind. She didn't regret having spoken out, but was glad to part on friendly terms. Over the next day or two something like normal communications resumed between her and Eliza, whom she truly loved – 'with all her faults, & she has many'. Yet she continued to compare Eliza's behaviour unfavourably with that of Lord and Lady Ilchester.

At the beginning of January 1816 Lady Ilchester gave birth to a son – 'the dear little Lord as they call him, a very fine boy'. Even then, Susan's thoughts turned to the absent one: 'How much pleasure would my dear O have had in this event — but it was not allowed him.' There was some anxiety over the new-born Lord Stavordale's breathing, but as the weeks passed he grew stronger. On 28 February Lord Ilchester, whose birthday it was, came into his aunt's room while she was dressing. When he left, her maid Carter remarked, 'It's a pleasure to look at Lord and Lady Ilchester, they look so happy and good — I hope this young Lord may be like them' – which exactly reflected her mistress's sentiments.

To leave such a scene of contentment and return to the house of desolation was almost more than Susan could bear, but she went to Stinsford the next day, when Melbury was once again filling up with guests. On 8

March she wrote to Eliza, 'I feel my return to this place more than I expected. My meals are dreadfull to me, I cannot describe the feel of sitting down by myself, & the vacant place opposite — but I will not dwell on sensations I am struggling from morning till night to conquer — at least to a great degree. I am at times cheerfull, & always endeavour to be so to those who have call'd upon me. You know pretty well who they are, good & kindly intention'd but nothing very agreeable. No Pitts at home…' (Among the conflicting feelings that complicated Susan's relationship with Eliza was envy — envy of her access to circles from which she herself was excluded. So in their correspondence she tended to downplay the kind of company available to her in rural Stinsford in comparison to the glittering possibilities available to Eliza in London, while at the same time making it clear that she considered her niece something of a slave to fashion.)

In an attempt to fill the vacant place opposite she occupied herself by reading over the letters she'd received in the early days of her marriage – '& from those [she noted in her journal], even from them that hated *him*, nothing can be extracted but praise & esteem - & yet what narrow principles, what love of power, what a distrust do they always shew of us. Without it, without the mad prejudices about America, how much less money placed properly & liberally should I have cost my family, than what I have done by droplets & presents that could never make us happy or take off poor Mr OB's feeling of being a burthen to them & yet not able to try any thing for himself while youth & health would have allow'd it — but kept in that banishment — Alas! Alas! how difficult it is to make others happy by the feelings of those who dispose of it — tho the feelings & intentions may be kind, & tho at last every thing turn'd out & has ended better than our expectations as to circumstances, how much time & anxiety would have been spared by earlier more liberal & more judicious exertions.'

However true this may be, in criticising her family (and particularly her uncle Holland) Susan makes no allowance for O'Brien's want of initiative or her own refusal to apologise for causing them so much distress. To the question Lord Holland had frequently posed — what else would she have him do? – she'd had no answer except to push for a grander governmental post than it was in his power to obtain for O'Brien.

And looking back over O'Brien's sporadic attempts to forge a career for himself once the stage (on which he had flourished) had been ruled out, was Susan herself entirely blameless? Had she not been so rigid over what he might do and where they should live, he might have stood a better chance of success when he finally took the plunge and studied for the bar at Lincoln's

Inn. This had been a tough enough assignment at his advanced age without the additional burden of his wife's unrelenting opposition. Her love of Stinsford and determination that he assume the mantle of a country gentleman prevailed, but at what cost? It is ironic that, following his demise, she should now be experiencing the very same feelings of purposelessness and uselessness that had driven him to make that last — one might say, desperate — attempt to forge a second career for himself, independent of his wife's influential friends.

Susan's journal provides ample evidence of the intensity and durability of her grief and mourning. She was much taken with 'some beautiful verses of Lord Byron's' and could not understand how 'any one that can write with such tender & amiable feeling can be so bad, so worse than bad a man'. She transcribed passages from *Childe Harold's Pilgrimage* and from other poems that found an echo in her current situation, such as 'And Thou art Dead, as Young and Fair':

> The better days of life were ours;
>   The worst can be but mine:
> The sun that cheers, the storm that lowers
>   Shall never more be thine.

But perhaps the most apposite lines Susan transcribed into her commonplace book at this time came not from the work of Byron but from that of a lesser poet, George Crabbe:

> … When our friends we lose
> Our alter'd feelings alter too our views;
> What in their tempers teaz'd us or distress'd,
> Is with our anger and the dead at rest
> And much we grieve no longer trial made
> For that impatience sometimes we display'd.
> Now to their love and worth of ev'ry kind,
> A soft compunction turns the afflicted mind;
> Virtues neglected then, ador'd become,
> And graces slighted, *blossom on the tomb.*

This — from *The Borough*, Letter 2 'The Church' – was the only verse of Crabbe's she transcribed (stressing the last four words), so she must have found it peculiarly apt, reminding her of her irritation with O'Brien in his last years over his resignation from the lucrative county receivership for which he was so ill-suited.

However profound her love for O'Brien, there does seem to be something willed about it. For a woman of principle, as she undoubtedly was, nothing short of a grand passion could warrant her original sin of defying her parents' wishes and marrying a man whom they, and all their peers, regarded as entirely unsuitable. What she had written to Lady Sarah, on hearing of her intention to re-marry – 'there was a propriety in your retreat, & a dignity annex'd to the idea of *one great passion*, tho' unfortunately placed, that gratified your friends & silenced your enemies' – not only reflected how she felt (and wanted others to feel) about her own marriage but also lay behind her disapproval of second marriages.

But if suffering in widowhood be the measure of the love between a man and a woman, there can be no question of the depth of her attachment to O'Brien. In a libidinous age when, in the aristocratic circles in which Susan moved, producing heirs to family fortunes was of far greater importance than marital fidelity, she and O'Brien seem to have lived a morally blameless, if physically barren, life. Her task during his lifetime had been to fight for his acceptance both in her own family and in the 'World' beyond, meaning the aristocratic world. Now that he had gone, she would find at least some of the purpose missing from her life in celebrating their marriage both in the pages of her journal (which was now her sole confidant) and in the memorial she was determined to erect to him — and in due course, herself — in Stinsford church. In both these activities she had half an eye to posterity — for though she wrote for herself and certainly not for publication, she hoped (and believed) that future generations of her family might be interested in their story.

9
THE RESTORATION OF A PICTURE

On the first anniversary of O'Brien's death the Floyers were due to dine with Susan, but she put them off, telling them she couldn't face any company, not even theirs, on that day. Surely, she wrote in her journal, 'there can be no harm in giving up *one day* to indulge sorrow without restraint.'

To avoid spending the anniversary of O'Brien's funeral at Stinsford, she accepted an invitation to stay at Abbotsbury. But on 9 September itself she was too upset to go downstairs for breakfast, recalling 'that day when like a second death I forever saw that all was over — even ceremony'. She did not tell anyone why she kept to her room, and 'none recollected the day of the Funeral they [had] attended'. There was a violent storm and no one went out, but Susan avoided attention by remaining upstairs.

Soon, however, she was participating fully in Abbotsbury life, 'sailing on the Fleet, in the Gig jumbling, on my feet trudging', as she would write to Eliza, '& in short doing every thing I did formerly, but I cannot say with the same ease, & I now *feel* that Abbotsbury requires youth & strength to enjoy it properly.' In her journal she elaborated: 'I did not think I could have done so much — my strength is still greater than I expected or desire. I shall I fear live till others are as tired of me as I so often am of myself.'

While at Abbotsbury, she read Benjamin Constant's *Adolphe* and, as she told Eliza, was very impressed: 'if Books ever are of use, this one may [be].' She was so moved by Adolphe's response to Ellénore's death in the last chapter that she drew Eliza's attention to the short passage beginning, *Naguère toutes mes actions...*

> Formerly, all my actions had an aim; I was sure that each one would either spare a pain or cause a pleasure; of this I had complained; I had been irritated that a friendly eye should observe my movements, that the happiness of

– 128 –

9 The Restoration of a Picture

William O'Brien: a print taken from Francis Cotes' portrait, 1760s.

another should be attached to them. No one now observed them; they interested nobody; no one contended with me for my time nor my hours; no voice called me back when I went out. I was free indeed; I was no longer loved. I was a stranger to all the world. [26]

Susan didn't expect Eliza to be as affected by this as she was, but said she could

---

[26] This *roman à clef*, based on Constant's love affair with Madame de Stael and written in a fortnight in 1807, was not published until 1816. After Napoleon's defeat at Waterloo, Constant left Paris and, early in 1816, gave a series of readings of his unpublished novella in London. These were so successful that he decided to publish it simultaneously in London and Paris. On 17 August 1816 (barely a month before Susan read *Adolphe*), he wrote to a cousin: 'I only published the thing to save myself the trouble of reading it in company. Having given four readings in a single week, I thought it would be more worthwhile to allow others to have the trouble of reading it for themselves.' (Cited by Harold Nicolson in his Introduction to the Signet Classic edition of *Adolphe and the Red Notebook*, 1959)

'bitterly vouch' for the 'truth of every sentiment'. So much so that she found it impossible to read the book downstairs for fear of breaking down in company. In her journal she noted that every day provided her with fresh instances of the questions she, like Adolphe, used to hear, but did no longer: 'nobody now asks me where I am going, when I come again &c &c.'

Returning to Stinsford had become an ordeal and this time was no exception; she was 'sadly again overcome in those scenes that I used to find so cheerfull'. By 20 September 1816 she recognised that the time had come to 'change my mourning'; she knew the servants should leave off theirs, but was reluctant to change anything: 'It is again like finishing — as if there had been no master.'

On Michaelmas day, while Susan was at church, a violent gale broke off the main branch of the plane tree that was the 'Glory of the Garden'. It had been O'Brien's favourite, as well as hers; indeed, he had planted it and had always maintained that if anything ever happened to it, 'he should hate the place'. For that reason, as she wrote to Eliza, it was some consolation that she was 'the only mourner for its misfortune'. Another consolation was that her nephew Harry was on hand to advise her on how best to conserve what remained of the tree, though it would never again provide the deep shade she cherished in summer and would be vulnerable to further storms — as was demonstrated two months later, when another branch was ripped off.

During November she had little or no company. She called this an experimental month in which she tried out living on her own, as she would have to do more and more, and was surprised to find it less unbearable than she'd feared it might be, even in winter. She was much preoccupied with O'Brien's memorial in the church, which was to take the form of a tablet; thinking of the future, she favoured the idea of two medallions, with hers to be put up 'at the time requir'd'. But lacking the skill to draw she was frustrated by her inability to transfer on to paper what was in her mind.

She went to Melbury before Christmas and remained there till the following April. Much as she enjoyed the stimulus of young company and tried to keep abreast of the times, she was living more and more in the past. On 15 February 1817 she wrote in her journal, 'In very bad spirits — sat & read all the morning to avoid talking on subjects I don't understand — but felt quite unamusable by any thing. These feels come over me sadly often, but in general I suppress them till night — truly I may say I water my couch with tears - & have I not unceasing cause to do so.' The presence of her niece Mary and family was balm to her troubled soul. As O'Brien's 'greatest favorite & friend, to whom he imparted his little grievances, & whose conversation & reasoning always sooth'd his mind', Mary was the relative from whom she derived the most comfort and support at this time.

Back at Stinsford in May, Susan had to do without her maid Carter, who went to Bath for medical treatment, which was an inconvenience — but nothing compared to what 'the loss of a valuable life' would be. She was not left entirely on her own; Miss Wightwick had come from her home in Somerton to stay and Susan's niece and namesake (one of her youngest brother Charles's numerous offspring) was also on duty as companion to her bereaved aunt. Neither would have appreciated what an irritable Susan, suffering from rheumatism and limping badly, recorded in her journal.

Their presence, she wrote, made the house feel more occupied and her meals less solitary, but their conversation neither amused her nor added 'much to any information but that of a perfect knowledge of the weak side of all the good folks of Wells & Somerton — next week I hope to have all their perfections'. But next week, she noted, was 'another week of *Ditto repeated* as the Americans used to say'. On the other hand she did appreciate Miss Wightwick's sterling qualities and found her 'a great resource to me in various respects in Carter's absence'.

One sultry summer evening Susan sat outside on the steps – 'can never do so without a pang — but what do I do without one? Walking by the room every night, even my own room — but I must not yield — my term is not yet come.' She was galvanised by the receipt of a letter from Lord Ilchester in London, telling her that the marble memorial tablet was finished and on its way to her. But when the day came to put it up there were so many workmen in the church that she took fright and left it to her brother Charles, who had been a good friend to O'Brien and was, after all, a vicar, to direct operations. On 2 August Lord Ilchester called in person and settled the craftsman's account with Susan (she doesn't say who paid what, but it's likely that Harry acted with his usual generosity). He 'pleas'd the Floyers very much by riding up to speak to them as they were passing at some distance — what a small attention from *great people* wins people's hearts! & how usefull it is on many occasions!'

Miss Wightwick remained with Susan for the first few days of September, and now, with Susan's thoughts focused solely on 'my lost friend', whom Miss W remembered well and respected highly, her conversational shortcomings were forgotten: 'no other person would suit me so well.' And on the 8th, when Miss Wightwick left Stinsford, it was with genuine regret that Susan saw her go: 'I shall miss her much, quiet, sensible & much attach'd to the family she pass'd so much of her youth with. She has shewn great attention & kindness to me during her long visit & I feel oblig'd to her for it. If I am ill she will come again at any time.'

Not long after O'Brien's death Susan had opened the case in which Francis Cotes's portrait of him had been stored, with the intention of putting the picture (the one that had caused so much heartache in their youth) on display. She had been horrified to discover the glass broken and the painting itself — she called it Cotes's masterpiece, 'which he had destin'd for the Academy' – seriously damaged. She determined to have it restored.

With this in mind, as well as to see old friends, she set out for London on 14 February 1818, two days after her seventy-fifth birthday. She stayed overnight at Farnham and arrived at Richmond, where the park was 'full of carriages & Horsemen, gay & beautiful', the next afternoon. But her heart sank, as it usually did, on approaching London: 'I could not help crying today — since February 1764 I have not enter'd London with hope or pleasure — that arrival decided my fate — after it was decided, the country has ever been my pleasure, my amusement.' She showed O'Brien's damaged portrait to a Mr and Mrs Frankland, with whom she had discussed restoring it a year earlier at Melbury, and they kindly undertook the task of finding an artist competent to do it.

The friend she most wanted to see in London was Lady Sarah, 'with whom I may talk of my lost friend, & of those days of anxiety (I must not say happiness, as fear exceeded hope) which no other knew, or can understand'. Sarah was now totally blind and, as Susan had written to Eliza years before, 'I do not write very often to her, as others read her letters, & then answering them, which she does at great length, must be troublesome.'

She found Lady Sarah much altered in appearance, but not 'in interest or in the stile of her conversation'. Over the next two months — for Susan ended up staying in town far longer than she'd intended — she and Sarah had many long conversations 'on her & my affairs both in ancient & modern times'. The emotional storms both had experienced in their lives were over and Sarah was 'happy in the society of a numerous & affectionate family', while Susan basked in the memory of '50 years of happy & unalter'd attachment to the most amiable of men'. She was particularly glad to spend her wedding anniversary with the one person who could remember the actual occasion and appreciate just what she had lost: 'Had she met with such a prize in the marriage lottery, how happy would her amiable quallitys have render'd her life!'

Their conversations ranged over all the old themes, the King's infatuation with Sarah — which Susan now felt was reciprocated far more than Sarah had ever let on before — Lord Holland's mismanagement of the affair, Susan's great love of O'Brien and what that had stirred up in the family and beyond, as well as Charles James Fox and his neglect of his early friends. Sarah said it was very characteristic of him 'to dislike & to avoid persons that he thought were discontented whether with him or otherwise — that he hated to see discontent, or hear complaints; & as his actions often occasion'd it to many, he constantly neglected & avoided them.' When his admiration and pursuit of Lady Crewe turned to indifference and neglect and she took him to task over it, he'd coolly responded, 'One folly was never sufficient for me.'

Susan was reminded of a remark Lady Crewe's mother Frances Greville had made to her about Charles when she was at Winterslow, after she and O'Brien had returned from America. Mrs Greville had said: 'If he had married you we should not have had all this ruinous gaming.' Susan very much doubted that. In her journal, she writes that she had seen 'in a nearer relation, with an Angel of a Wife, that this miserable propensity is not to be conquer'd without a stronger resolution than C Fox ever shew'd in the concerns of his life' – referring, of course, to her brother, the 2nd Earl of Ilchester, an Eton contemporary as well as a cousin of Charles Fox.

Thinking of Charles strengthened her conviction that 'for heart, honor & every virtue I shall always think I chose the best'. Sarah agreed, telling her how much she'd always liked O'Brien, 'who never complain'd or appear'd discontented'. But Susan knew how much of that was due to pride, and what an effort it cost him in relation to Charles Fox, 'for he often came home to me almost broken-hearted with disappointment & anger at his unfeeling behavior'.

When she wasn't reminiscing with Sarah, Susan spent most of her time with one or other of her nieces, Eliza, or Mary, or Louisa Lansdowne. One April evening at a party at Lansdowne House – 'very brilliant with court dresses, finery & feathers' – she was just entering into the spirit of the occasion when a country acquaintance, Mrs Bankes of Kingston Lacy, called out to her, 'Gayest of the Gay, I see.' Susan was mortified. A line of Lord Byron's that had been going through her head ever since she'd come to London – 'too deeply rested there to vanish' – instantly came to mind and shattered 'the illusion dissipation & company had occasion'd'. Her evening was ruined.

She didn't go out the next day but brooded on Mrs Bankes's wounding remark, thinking how unfair it was, how little she deserved the name of Gayest of the Gay, how the appeal of London 'transactions' was diminishing daily and how she had probably overstayed her welcome. Though everyone had been kind to her, they could not possibly want her there, since she was 'neither usefull or ornamental'. She had no reason to prolong her stay in town. The precious picture of O'Brien had been beautifully restored and would be despatched to Stinsford, where she too was ready to go.

Once she got home, she suffered a reaction: 'there is a buoyancy in London that like the sea water keeps one up, in spite of nerves, of heart, of every thing, one's very being is confused — but when that ceases, regrets, loss, solitude, inutillity, every thing returns with double pressure, & sinks one to the very depth.'

Worse was to follow. After all the trouble she'd taken to get O'Brien's picture restored, it arrived at Stinsford as badly damaged as it had been before. Though it had been packed with great care, the transport wagon in which it came had overturned on the road, throwing out the picture, smashing both frame and glass and injuring the painting itself. While Susan thought it might still be possible to repair it, she could hardly impose on the Franklands' good nature again and who was to say it wouldn't suffer another accident? If only she had the talent to restore the portrait herself.

'I am griev'd, embarrass'd & almost craz'd,' she wrote – 'I only wish'd to get this dear Picture, which I think I love the better for all its misfortunes, made perfect as it was at first, when it was as like as ever was a picture, & what Coats [sic] said was the best he had ever painted.'

In London she'd felt satisfied with what she'd had done for the picture — that and the plaque she'd put up in Stinsford church had completed all she had left to do in her life. Now with the picture she would have to start all over again.

But at Melbury the following month, she spoke to a family friend and fellow guest, Rev. Townshend Selwyn, who was confident he could do the job. So Susan sent home for the picture, 'tho fearfull of another journey for it'. It arrived safely and 'with great skill & success it is once more restor'd'. She took it back with her to Stinsford, where she hung it in the library – '& in that room I hope to pass much of the remaining time I have to live'.

10
A Prodigy

Susan outlived her husband by twelve years — years in which she felt increasingly isolated by age and the loss of loved ones. No sooner had her ailing friend and neighbour Mrs Pitt died than another dear neighbour, Rev. Floyer, suffered a paralytic stroke. Lady Sarah, she heard, had also been paralysed by a stroke. Floyer lasted little more than a year, but Sarah, already blind, her memory gone, survived in an almost vegetable state for another eight years.

A year after Mrs Pitt's death Morton Pitt married again. Susan, though she disapproved of second marriages, made an exception in his case; she'd been fond of the first Mrs Pitt but knew the marriage had not been a happy one. Of the second Mrs Pitt she wrote to Eliza, 'It's a cousin of Lord Rivers, six &

Holland House, *c.*1752.

thirty, very musical, but not *belle*...' Not long after the marriage the Pitts had twins. Susan's friendship with Mr Pitt remained strong, but she didn't have the same intimate relationship with the second family that she and O'Brien had had with the first.

At her age deaths of contemporaries were only to be expected; but untimely deaths were another matter. When Caroline, Lady Ilchester, having produced a son and heir, died in giving birth to a second son, it was not just a tragedy for Susan's beloved Harry, who was only thirty-two (and would never remarry); it affected the whole family. And some years later, when young William Floyer, sailing home from Plymouth after his first tour at sea in the Navy, drowned off Portland Bill, Susan was devastated. She had grown very close to the widowed Mrs Floyer, who now had to bury her elder son alongside his father.

Before the Rev. Floyer had been struck down, Susan had had a conversation with him on whether departed spirits 'could know, approve or otherwise of what those still living did or felt on their account'. He'd said that one authority had advised a lady who'd lost her husband that she 'should behave as if seen and judg'd by him' and had waxed so enthusiastic on the subject that Susan couldn't help but exclaim, 'That's what I do every day of my Life.'

She continued to do that. But she was doubtful about the possibility of being reunited with O'Brien after death, though it was her fondest wish. She continued, too, to regard the first two days of September as sacred to his memory. Their life together had been full of 'disappointments, privations & poverty', but she could never have been happy with anyone else. Where they had differed she had 'generally found his judgment better than my own & his principles & actions were such as confirm'd & strengthen'd every virtuous inclination or instruction I had ever receiv'd'.

Nevertheless his decision to resign the county receivership — a decision she had so bitterly opposed — came back to haunt her long after he had gone. As she'd predicted, the longer she lived the more Walter Hodges resented the contract which obliged him to make annual payments to her that he could ill-afford. When he first sounded her out on putting an end to this arrangement, Susan was in a dilemma: 'I must either refuse a needy mans unreasonable request, or involve myself in the unpleasant circumstances I am but just reliev'd from.' But refuse him she did, arguing that any money she managed to put aside during the remainder of her life was destined for her brother Charles's family, which was quite as large and needy as Mr Hodges's and had a far greater claim on her.

Yet she was uneasy about this decision. She consulted John Francis

Browne, ex-MP for the county of Dorset and one of the signatories of the bond securing the annuity, when he visited her some months later, and was relieved to find that he endorsed her action. But that was by no means the end of the matter, which would hang over the remaining years of her life just as it had clouded the last years of her marriage.

In 1820 the receiver-generalship attracted the attention of a parliamentary committee that included the radical politician Joseph Hume. In early June Susan received a panicky and 'very unpleasant' note from Mr Hodges, in which he wrote that he was expecting to be suspended and that the trouble stemmed from the agreement he'd made with O'Brien. Three days later, he called in person. He had learned that Hume's committee was investigating *all* receivers-general, not just him, though the agreement with O'Brien was indeed known about. He seemed 'pretty easy' and Susan was relieved.

But the following month she got another letter from him, enclosing one he had received from Mr Winter at the Tax Office in London, raising the question of the annuity and 'threatening the loss of his place if he continues it'. Browne happened to be visiting her when she got this letter and she showed it to him. Though he conceded that the annuity was to cease only in the event of Hodges's death, and 'that no other contingency was contemplated', he gave it as his opinion that the legality of such an agreement had now been called into question. But Susan clung to the hope that Browne, 'a worthy man', would 'not let a quirk of law or even of power operate upon his mind when he must know the clear meaning of the whole agreement'.

What was at stake was almost a third of her income and Susan was unwilling to renounce that. Apart from any practical considerations, she knew how important the agreement had been to O'Brien and felt strongly that his wishes should be honoured. She replied to Hodges to that effect, having first consulted with her niece Harriot and Harriot's husband James Frampton, as well as her brother Charles when he visited. Charles told her he'd seen Browne, 'who did not speak of the business in the manner he expected about the Bond'. Susan thought her brother should have made more of such an opening – 'but every one seems afraid of Browne'.

Morton Pitt tried to intercede with Hodges and was shown another letter from the Tax Office with a number of 'rather extraordinary querys', the last of which was, how much would he do the business for? Hodges had replied, that must be left to the officials' liberality – 'a bad word now,' Susan reckoned, '& as much abus'd as its fellow word Liberty is.' The next day, dining at the Framptons, she met Wollaston and, since he had been involved in the original negotiations with Hodges both as a lawyer and as a friend, showed him the most recent letters. She found him reluctant to be drawn into the dispute, and thought he was 'visibly afraid of any thing that may displease or vex Browne' – whom she no longer considered a worthy man or even a friend. She hoped she might be mistaken but she foresaw 'no good either from the Law or the Honor of my Bond or my Bondsmen'.

In August, Wollaston called on her and offered to arbitrate if, in Susan's words, 'all the securitys desire it — *which they will not do*'. She reminded him of a letter he had written when the agreement was being made, but he didn't want to know: 'he forgets every thing past — altogether lukewarm.' She feared she would be 'the dupe'.

When the banker Pattison called, she asked him about the parliamentary committee to which he'd been summoned to give evidence. He said the chairman had asked him if anything had been paid by Hodges, and he'd replied that he knew 'nothing but what was quite confidential'. At which point Mr Hume 'sprang up, & insisted that... he must answer what & how, which he did'. Hence the uncomfortable situation Hodges now found himself in vis-à-vis the Tax Office. Pattison confirmed that Hodges had nothing to offer or give and Susan said she was reluctant to press him for what she was owed. Despite her doubts about Wollaston, she dropped a hint that he might be the man to consult if a compromise was to be reached.

At Abbotsbury for a few days in September, she took the opportunity of discussing the matter with Harriot Frampton, who urged her to trust Wollaston to do the right thing. But she was not persuaded: 'to what avail opinions, where there is visibly a fear of offending the unjust party & little zeal for the just. They talk of an Arbitration but when an instrument is declar'd by one lawyer to be invalid why shew it to another? It is the circumstances, not the legality that can signify. It's only plaguing me with a little more of their special pleading.'

Both Mr Frampton and her brother Charles professed astonishment and Charles offered to write to Browne. But Susan reiterated that it would come to nothing. Further visits to Stinsford from Wollaston failed to reassure Susan, who wrote of him, 'he is not my enemy — but such a cold friend is sometimes worse.' And though the business rumbled on for months, the end was never in doubt.

The cessation of the annuity that was supposed to have been paid for the remainder of Susan's life only added to her feeling of having outlived her time. What upset her most was that some of her nearest and dearest — in particular, her brother Charles and her niece Harriot — seemed keener on retaining the friendship of Browne than on obtaining justice for her. But she tried hard to suppress such thoughts.

Despite her straitened circumstances, on 8 April 1825 the eighty-two-year-old Susan made a final foray to London with the express purpose of 'visiting for the last time my earliest & dearest friend who is almost in a dying state'. Yet once she was in London, she put off seeing Lady Sarah for three weeks — during which time she was fêted by her nieces Eliza and Louisa and her cousins Caroline Fox and the 3rd Lord Holland.

When she did see Sarah, she was appalled: 'a greater decay of Nature can not be — alas! what a lesson! & yet what can it teach us — we can not prevent the loss of sight — we cannot prevent the loss of memory — we can only endeavour to bear with all the patience & fortitude nature will allow us what nothing can prevent.' Observing Sarah's state, she feared for her own future: her eyesight was beginning to fail and she was having difficulty in walking; all she could do was pray 'to be removed before these ills increase & accumulate'. The last time she had seen her old friend, they had talked at great length, over several days, of their shared past. Sarah was beyond that now.

Susan was soon caught up again in the social whirl for which, Sarah had once told her, she was 'formed by nature'. She attended a large dinner party at Holland House and for the first time in over sixty years was invited to stay in the place that had been the scene of Sarah's and her youthful romantic and theatrical escapades, no longer *persona non grata* but a relic of a bygone age, a living legend, a 'prodigy' according to Lord William Russell (younger brother of Lord John Russell and habitué of Holland House), her longevity celebrated in a — bad — poem by Lord Holland in imitation of a better one by Sir Charles Hanbury Williams welcoming her into the world in her infancy.

In fashionable Holland House she encountered several Whig grandees she had never met before, as well as some of the intellectuals whose patron Lord Holland was, including the 'Spaniard de Blanco' (Joseph Blanco White) and John Allen, a doctor by training, now mainly remembered as a contributor to the *Edinburgh Review*, Lord Holland's amanuensis and a key member of the Holland House set. A republican in theory, Allen was — in Lord Holland's words – 'the most liberal of men towards those of all opinions'.

Caroline Fox, who was a sympathetic and amused spectator of Susan's stay at Holland House, wrote:

> Sixty-two years had passed over her head since she had last slept under that old roof, and two generations of persons dear to her had disappeared from the face of the earth. Food enough for melancholy you will allow, but she shook it off after the first hour, and, retaining all the quickness and cleverness of her youthful conversation, she pleased and was pleased with all she saw and heard, and with surprising readiness entered into the topics of the day and the tone and character of the persons she met, as if she had lived all her life among them. But for certain Tory sentiments which she made no scruple of uttering, I think at 83 [sic] she would have made a conquest of Mr Allen.

※

Lady Sarah died on 26 August 1826, and Susan wrote: 'She is gone; I never loved any one so well — I shall soon follow her.' But not as soon as she had come to wish. She survived her dearest friend by almost a year.

She spent her last Christmas at Melbury, where she found 'all the Talbots' – by which she meant her nieces Eliza and Mary and all their children, be they Talbots or Feildings (Eliza having had two daughters with Capt. Feilding, half-sisters to William Henry Fox Talbot). It was a lively gathering; the children, both boys and girls, were 'charming & promising'; yet Susan felt out of it.

'I have plenty of Nieces,' she wrote, 'but alas! I have but little enjoyment of their society. That is one of the adversitys of age — young ones are afraid of you — the Old cannot help one another, & the mid's tend so much towards the young that they sometimes fancy they still belong to that description of persons. However, having neither children or grandchildren I must suffer that mortification from 20 to 80 — Fate's decrees are hard & often very unaccountable.'

Never before had Susan expressed on paper her regret that her marriage to O'Brien had been childless; in her journal, she complained of many — often trivial — things, but never of that. Not until the very end of her life did she let on how much it hurt, though the fact that she treated Eliza more as a surrogate daughter than a niece testifies to a lifelong yearning for a child, or children, of her own.

Though her life was ebbing away, she never ceased thinking of O'Brien and almost the last entry in her journal (for 13 June 1827) reads: '... I pass'd the evening in the garden, on the Gravel Walk — no interruptions — the finest evening possible — indulging reflexions on the many pass'd there in happiness & society now gone — Darby & Joan we were often call'd — but now only the Old & *triste* Joan remains to sit & view the last habitation she can remove to, hoping & praying to be again united, in the same tomb.'

She died on 9 August. Her brother Charles and nephew Harry ensured that the wishes she had often expressed with regard to her memorial in Stinsford church were carried out. She was buried beside her husband in a vault made 'just large enough for our two selves only'; and a matching plaque, of design and wording approved by her, was erected next to his, linked by two hearts and inscribed

TO THE MEMORY OF
SUSANNA SARAH LOUISA
ELDEST DAUGHTER OF
STEP^N. FIRST EARL OF ILCHESTER
OB. AUGUST 9. 1827
AET. 83

OF

WILLIAM O BRIEN, ESQ^{RE}.
THE FAITHFUL WIFE
AND
INSEPARABLE COMPANION.

There was just one small error — her age. Susan was eighty-four, not eighty-three, when she died. This begs the question, had she been so convinced she would not survive 1826 that she wrote in her age then and no one had thought to correct it, or did her nearest relatives simply miscalculate? Either way, one can confidently assert that Susan, a stickler for accuracy in so important a matter as her memorial, would not have been best pleased.

It is appropriate that one of Lady Susan's Dorset neighbours should have the last word. Mary Frampton was a sister-in-law of Susan's niece Harriot. She never married but was a skilled botanist and floral artist who left five volumes of plant drawings, as well as a journal. What she writes there of the couple she knew may serve as an epitaph:

> They remained always most affectionately attached to each other. Lady Susan was a woman of a very strong and highly improved understanding, extremely agreeable in society, a steady, warm-hearted friend, and a person in whose conversation anything like gossip or abuse of your neighbour never held a place, but to the very latest hour of her existence her lofty character was most strongly marked. Her principles and education, as well as her husband's, had been neglected; but whatever their errors might be, in both they were redeemed by very valuable and amiable qualities, and no two people were more liked or their society more courted in the middle and close of their lives. He had the most amenity [in the archaic sense of 'agreeability'], she most strength of character. *Requiescant in pace.*'

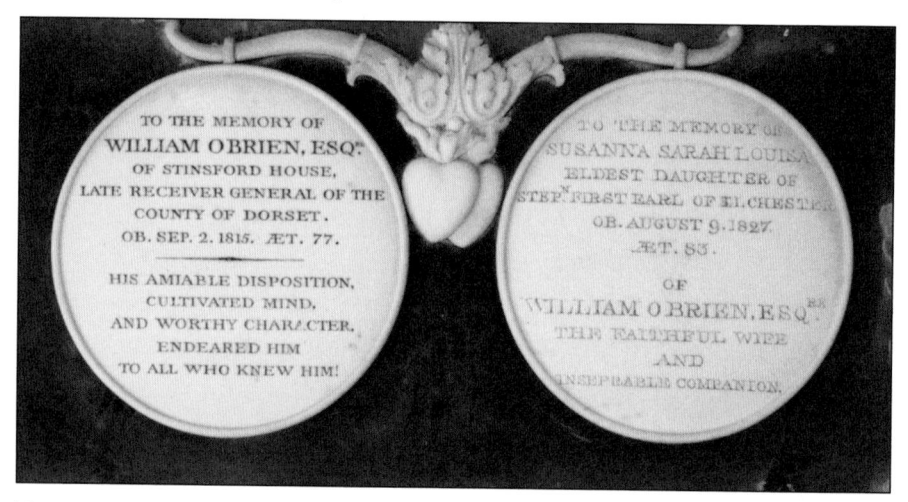

The couple's memorial tablet in Stinsford Church.

Acknowledgements

This book has had a long gestation period, and my earliest debt is to the staff of the Manuscripts reading room of the British Library. This became my work place for a few years, while I trawled through all the Holland House papers relating to Lady Susan and her immediate family and many other documents and books. Everyone there was unfailingly courteous and helpful – as well as tolerant of the occasional beep-beep noise when I had to back my mobility scooter out of a tricky corner.

I am very grateful to the following friends who read and commented on one or other of the many drafts of the book: Sarah Bakewell, Beryl Gray and Paula Lichtarowicz. John Orbell, Julia Sheppard, the Hon. Mrs Charlotte Townshend and her assistant, Laura Baterip, have also given me invaluable help and support along the way. Many thanks, too, to David Burnett of the Dovecote Press for agreeing to publish the book under his imprint and for all his practical help and advice in carrying this through; to the indexer, Ildi Clarke, who stepped in at very short notice and did a marvellous job at very high speed; and to the photographer, Maisie Hill, who produced excellent images of some of the portraits reproduced in this book.

My greatest debt is to my old friend and former colleague, Tony Garrett, who spared no effort in designing the book and the cover not just once but twice over. His skill and professionalism are exemplary, and his unfailing patience and good humour have sustained me throughout this process.

Finally, without the love and support of Jenny, my wife, who always believed in the potential of this story, I could not have completed writing it.

Illustration acknowledgements

Most of the illustrations were supplied by the owner of the images. The author and publisher are also grateful to the Albany Institute of History & Art for permission to reproduce Edward Lamson Henry's 1903 painting of Johnson Hall (Sir William Johnson Presenting Medals to the Indian Chiefs of the Six Nations at Johnstown, NY, 1772) and for supplying the image.

Sources

Manuscript Collections

The British Library:
    Holland House Papers
    Talbot Papers

The main source for this book is the Holland House Papers in the British Library, Add MSS 51337-51467 — particularly 51358-51362, which include Susan's unpublished journal (51359 & 51360), her correspondence, commonplace books and accounts, and O'Brien's verses and other writings, as well as his correspondence. Lady Susan's letters to her niece Lady Elizabeth Fox Strangways/Talbot/Feilding are also in the British Library among the recently acquired Fox Talbot archive.

Published Works

The letters between Lady Sarah Lennox and Lady Susan (though it's mainly Sarah's side of the correspondence that has survived) were published in 1902 under the title, *The Life and Letters of Lady Sarah Lennox 1745-1826*, edited by the then Countess of Ilchester and her son Lord Stavordale.

The Journal of Mary Frampton, from the year 1779, until the year 1846, edited by Harriot Georgiana Mundy and published in 1885, is something of a ragbag, or treasure trove, of 'various interesting and curious letters, anecdotes, &c', relating to Dorset and beyond at that time.

George Selwyn and His Contemporaries, edited by John Heneage Jesse and published in 1841, contains interesting contemporary letters, many of them written to Selwyn by the Earl of Carlisle about Charles James Fox.

Memoirs of the Colman Family, edited by Richard Brinsley Peake and published in 1841, Thomas Davies's *Memoirs of the Life of David Garrick Esq*, published in 1781, and John Genest's *Some Account of the English Stage from the Restoration in 1660 to 1830* (Vols IV & V), 1832, all give accounts of O'Brien's career as an actor and, briefly, playwright.

The most useful secondary source for the Fox-Strangways family in this period is Joanna Martin's well-researched *Wives and Daughters: Women and Children in the Georgian Country House* (2004), which includes a chapter on Lady Susan and quotes extensively from her journal throughout the book.

Other invaluable recent books include Leslie Mitchell's excellent *Charles James Fox* (1992) and *The Whig World 1760-1837* (2005); Stella Tillyard's splendid *Aristocrats* (1994); and Fintan O'Toole's *A Traitor's Kiss: The Life of Richard Brinsley*

SOURCES

Sheridan (1997) and, more especially, his *White Savage: William Johnson and the Invention of America* (2005), which contributed greatly to my understanding of the America in which Susan and O'Brien spent their six-year exile. Charlotte Wilcoxen's pioneering essay, 'A Highborn Lady in Colonial New York' (1977) was also a considerable help to me in writing the chapters about the O'Briens' American experience.

REFERENCE NOTES

Abbreviations used in the references below
Add MSS (+ number) – British Library Additional Manuscripts
TP — the papers of Henry Fox Talbot and family in the British Library (in the process of being catalogued)
ODNB — Oxford Dictionary of National Biography
Ly SFS/SO'B — Lady Susan Fox Strangways/Susan O'Brien
WO'B — William O'Brien
Ly SL/SB/SN — Lady Sarah Lennox/Bunbury/Napier
HF/Ld H — Henry Fox/1st Lord Holland
Ly H — Lady Caroline Holland
Ld I — Stephen Fox, 1st Earl of Ilchester
Ly I — Elizabeth, Countess of Ilchester
HW — Horace Walpole
CU — Clotworthy Upton, later Baron Templeton
ST — Samuel Touchet MP
AD — Adam Drummond

Preface

7   'seen and admired', F Hardy, *The Early Life of Thomas Hardy*, p. 11
'make it just large...', *ibid*, p. 12
'when a boy chorister...', cited in C Tomalin, *Thomas Hardy*, p. 243
8   'lent the occupants...', F Hardy, *The Early Life of Thomas Hardy*, p. 11
'could not have believed...', HW to the Earl of Hertford, 12 Apr 1764, *The Letters of Horace Walpole, Earl of Orford*, vol iv, p. 405
'Though in these...', F Hardy, *The Early Life of Thomas Hardy*, p. 11
'The Noble...', see Thomas Hardy, *The Complete Poems*, pp. 289-295

Part 1: Elopement and Exile

15   'I am distracted...', WO'B to Ly SFS, undated (1763/4), Add MSS 51352

1. A Clandestine Wedding

17   'My Lady — my Lady...', Horace Walpole to the Earl of Hertford, 12 Apr 1764, *The Letters of Horace Walpole, Earl of Orford*, vol iv, p. 405
'I was infinitely...', HW to George Montagu, 22 Jan 1761, Lewis and Brown (eds.), *Horace Walpole's Correspondence with George Montagu*, p. 335
18   'Even a footman...', HW to Ld Hertford, 12 Apr 1764, *The Letters of Horace Walpole*, vol iv, pp. 404-05
'credulity and negligence', *ibid*
'Lady Susan was...', *ibid*
'under lock and key...', *ibid*
19   'Mr Fox fell in love...', Horace Walpole, cited in S Tillyard, *Aristocrats*, pp. 30-31
'He is a sweet man...', cited in Lord Ilchester, *The Home of the Hollands*, p.69
20   'the proudest of...', Mundy (ed), *the Journal of Mary Frampton*, p. 19

– 145 –

'I always thought...', David Garrick to the Duke of Devonshire, 25 June 1764, David M Little and George M Kahrl (eds), *The Letters of David Garrick*, vol I, p. 419

21 'The character of Brazen...', cited in Wm Stone Jr (ed), *The London Stage 1600-1800*, p. 886
'In elegance of...', Davies, *Memoirs of the Life of David Garrick, Esq*, vol I, pp. 270-271
'sink the player...', John Genest, *Some Account of the English Stage from the Restoration in 1660 to 1830*, vol iv, pp. 536-538

22 'Oh Lord, only...', Ly SL to Ly SFS, 24 Oct 1761, Ilchester & Stavordale (eds), *The Life & Letters of Lady Sarah Lennox 1745-1826*, vol 1, p. 114
'spirited good likeness', Ly SO'B to Ly E Feilding, 11 Oct 1808, TP

23 'he won't learn...', Ly SL to Ly SFS, 15 Dec 1761, Ilchester & Stavordale, *op. cit.*, p. 114
'will act...', HF to Ld I, 9 Jan 1762, Add MSS 51421
'in thinking that...', Ly SO'B's Journal, 10 Mar 1818, Add MSS 51360

24 'Lady Susan/April 6...', on back of Ly SFS to Ld H, Fri 6 Apr 1764, Add MSS 51352
'that base and treacherous...', Ld I to Ly SB, Sun 8 Apr 1764, Add MSS 51350
'Lady Suke is so...', HF to Ld I, 9 Jan 1762, Add MSS 51421

26 'son of a fencing...', Genest, *op. cit.*, vol iv, pp. 536-538
'was one of those...', WO'B's autobiographical note, 3 Aug 1808, Add MSS 51358

27 'a McCarty of the...', *ibid*
'I may be more...', *ibid*
'taken a good deal of...', Charlotte Digby to Ld H, 13 Apr 1764, Add MSS 51422

28 'Obrien the Player...', Boswell, *London Journal*, p. 217
'a scheme of this kind...', Adam Drummond to Ld H, 13 Sept 1764, Add MSS 51432

29 'I thought in his manner...', *ibid*
'I can't leave...', Ly SO'B to Ld H, 1 Sept 1764, Add MSS 51352
'hang'd at Tyburn', Ld H to Ly SO'B, 8 Mar 1765, Add MSS 51352
'in good health and...', ST to Ld H, 29 Sept 1764, Add MSS 51425

2. Merchants and Mohawks

30 'but between you and...', WO'B to George Garrick, 10 Nov 1764, cited in Highfill et al, *A Biographical Dictionary...*, Vol II, pp. 89-92
'Lady Susan I think...', CU to Ld H, 26 July 1764, Add MSS 51405
'very sick at my house...', ST to Ld H, 21 Aug 1764, Add MSS 51425
'I should rather think...', Ly I to Ld H, 8 Aug 1764, Add MSS 51421
'Your letters...', *ibid*

31 'the place to...', Lord Adam Gordon, 'Journal of an Officer's Travels in America and the West Indies 1764-1765', in Mereness (ed), *Travels in the American Colonies*, pp. 414-415
'Every thing appears...', WO'B to George Garrick, 10 Nov 1764, Highfill' *op. cit.*, Vol II, pp. 89-92
'barren & uncultivated', Ly SO'B to Ld H, 10 Nov 1764, Add MSS 51352
'the town is not...', Ly SO'B to Ly SB, cited in Charlotte Wilcoxen, 'A Highborn Lady in Colonial New York', *The New-York Historical Society Quarterly*, vol lxiii, No. 4, Oct 1979, p. 328
'be assured of every...', John Watts to James Napier, 28 Oct 1764, cited in Wilcoxen, *op. cit.*, p. 327
'do them all a service...', Oliver DeLancey to Adam Drummond, 8 Nov 1764, Add MSS 51432
'found them in the...', Lord Stirling (Wm Alexander) to AD, 6 Nov 1764, *ibid*

Sources

32   'the poor unhappy...', John Watts to James Napier, 28 Oct 1764, cited in Wilcoxen, *op. cit.*, p. 327
'a poor devil...', John Watts to Robert Monckton, 6 Nov 1764, *ibid*, p. 331
'poor Lady Susan...', AD to Ld H, 2 July 1765, Add MSS 51433
'one of the most thoughtless...', *ibid*
'Mr Croghan goes...', Ly SO'B to Ld H, 19 Aug 1764, Add MSS 51352

33   'Irish fiefdom', O'Toole, *White Savage*, p. 232
'granted long ago...', Ly SO'B to Ld H, 10 Nov 1764, Add MSS 51352
'purchasing of Lands...', Cadwallader Colden to Ld H, 5 Nov 1764, Add MSS 51432
'no one attempts...', Ly SO'B to Ld H, 10 Nov 1764, Add MSS 51352

34   'for my accounts...', Ly SO'B to Clotworthy Upton, 13 Apr 1765, Add MSS 51356
'my Lord Holland...', Samuel Touchet to Ly SO'B, 10 Nov 1764, *ibid*
'I thought we should never...', ST to Ld H, 29 Sept 1764, Add MSS 51425
'your father pay for...', Ly Sarah Bunbury to Ly SO'B, 4 Nov 1764, Ilchester & Stavordale, *The Life and Letters of Lady Sarah Lennox*, vol I, p. 148

35   'you are much too...', Ld I to Ld H, 24 Nov 1764, Add MSS 51421
'he saw no prospect...', ST to Ly SO'B, 10 Nov 1764, Add MSS 51356
'an abandon'd...', Ly SO'B to Ld H, 21 Jan 1765, Add MSS 51352
'after all indeed...', *ibid*

36   'Dear Madam...', Ld H to Ly SO'B, 8 Mar 1765, Add MSS 51352

37   'as you say despair...', Ly SO'B to Ld H, 3 June 1765, Add Mss 51352
'I don't find Mr...', ST to Ly SO'B, 8 June 1765, Add MSS 51356

38   'Nothing can be more...', Ly SO'B's account of her journey from New York to Quebec, 1769, Add MSS 51359
'dull and ill built....', Journal of Lord Adam Gordon, Mereness, *op. cit.*, pp. 416-417

39   'no consideration...', *ibid*, pp. 417-418
'I have had Lord Adam...', Sir William Johnson to Cadwallader Colden, 20 June 1765, cited in Wilcoxen, *op. cit.*, p. 339
'the scion of a noble...', Wm L Stone, *The Life and Times of Sir William Johnson, Bart*, vol II, p. 243
'housekeeping among the...', cited in Wilcoxen, *op. cit.*, p. 339

40   'error... about land...', Ld H to Ly SO'B, 8 Mar 1765, Add MSS 51352
'General Gage & every...', Ly SO'B's margin comment on CU to Ly SO'B, 10 Aug 1765, Add MSS 51356
'A Newfoundlander to...', poem by WO'B, 1765, Add MSS 51361

41   'vastly diverted...', Ly SB to Ly SO'B, 9 Jan 1766, Ilchester & Stavordale, *op. cit.*, vol I, pp. 177-178
'a pink & green...', ditto, 8 May 1766, *ibid*, p. 195
'The new play of...', ditto, *ibid*, p. 190
'bring over some...', David Garrick to WO'B, 31 May 1766, Add MSS 51358

42   'take a peep...', WO'B to George Garrick, 10 Nov 1764, cited in Highfill et al, *op. cit.*, p. 91
'I have scolded...', D Garrick to WO'B, 31 May 1766, Add MSS 51358
'it's a beginning...', ST to WO'B, 14 Dec 1765, Add MSS 51356

43   'but I must have...', Ly SB to Ly SO'B, 8 May 1766, Ilchester & Stavordale, *op. cit.*, p. 191
'all your friends seem...', Ly I to Ly SO'B, circa 10 May 1766, Add MSS 51344
'with more Astonishment...', Journal of Lord Adam Gordon, Mereness, *op. cit.*, p. 425
'I know you delighted...', Ly SB to Ly SO'B, 7 July 1766, Ilchester & Stavordale, *op. cit.*, vol I, p. 198

'bore all the fattigues…', Lt Benjamin Roberts to Sir Wm Johnson, 3 July 1766, cited in Wilcoxen, *op. cit.*, p. 342
'gentleman that went…', Ly SB to Ly SO'B, 12 Feb 1768, Ilchester & Stavordale, *op. cit.*, vol I, p. 217

44 'your American…', ST to WO'B, 8 Feb 1766, Add MSS 51356
'your riotous Americans…', ditto, 8 Mar 1766, *ibid*
'these rebellions…', Ly SB to Ly SO'B, 9 Jan 1766, Ilchester & Stavordale, *op. cit.*, vol I, p. 184
'your nasty American…', ditto, 5 Feb 1766, *ibid*, p. 185
'I hope the Mother…', D Garrick to WO'B, 31 May 1766, Add MSS 51358
'just like a dying…', Ly I to Ly SO'B, 28 May 1766, Add MSS 51344
'I cannot give you…', Ly SB to Ly SO'B, 8 May 1766, Ilchester & Stavordale, *op. cit.*, vol I, p. 194
'entirely of his own…', Ld H to Ly SO'B, 10 Apr 1766, Add MSS 51532

45 ''tis a little blessed…', Ly SB to Ly SO'B, 8 May 1766, Ilchester & Stavordale, *op. cit.*, vol I, p. 193
'vastly sorry to find…', Ly SB to Ly SO'B, 9 Oct 1766, Ilchester & Stavordale, *op. cit.*, vol I, p. 200
'after this, my…', ditto, 26 Nov 1766, *ibid*, p. 205
'a perfect, happy…', *ibid*, p. 206

46 'you might be distressed…', ditto, 7 May 1767, *ibid*, p. 208
'"But Madam,"…', *ibid*, pp. 209-10
'and what your moderate…', Ld H to Ly SO'B, 12 June 1767, Add MSS 51532

47 'Ld H proposes to…', Ly I to Ly SO'B, 17 Oct 1767, Add MSS 51344
'not desire to vex…', Ly SB to Ly SO'B, 11 June 1768, Ilchester & Stavordale, *op. cit.*, vol I, pp. 220-221
'I have ask'd Lord H…', *ibid*, pp. 221-222
'No doubt much…', *ibid*, p. 223 (footnote)

48 'Lady Susan preserved…', Ilchester & Stavordale, *op. cit.*, p. 223
'kind, sensible…', Ly SB to Ly SO'B, 23 Oct 1767, *ibid*, pp. 213-214
'I dare say Lady Sarah's…', Ly I to Ly SO'B, 3 Apr 1769, Add MSS 51344

49 'obtained from…', ST to Ly SO'B, 7 May 1768, Add MSS 51356
'but cannot as yet…', CU to Ly SO'B, 11 May 1768, *ibid*
'a good house…', ST to Ly SO'B, 16 Sept 1768, *ibid*
'I dare say it will…', Ly I to Ly SO'B, 3 Apr 1768, Add MSS 51344
'and find by…', Ly SO'B to Ly H, 14 May 1769, Add MSS 51532

50 'On an American Spring…', poem by WO'B, 1768, Add MSS 51361
'several good…', Ly I to Ly SO'B, 18 June 1769, Add MSS 51344
'Neither respectable…', Ly SO'B's margin comment on ST to Ly SO'B, 16 Sept 1768, Add MSS 51356

51 'labouring to reform…', Horace Walpole, *Last Journals*, cited in Wilcoxen, *op. cit.*, p. 346
'an injudicious…', Ly SO'B's Journal, 14 Nov 1817, Add MSS 51360

Part 2: Attendance and Dependence

3. Stinsford

54 'Had I known…', Ly SO'B's Journal, 1770, Add MSS 51359
'As long as my…', Ly Harriot to Ly SO'B, 9 Feb 1771, Add MSS 51357
'As I never receive…', Ly SO'B to Ly H Acland, 11 Feb 1771, Add MSS 51357

55 'the mortifications of…', Ly SO'B's Journal, 1771, Add MSS 51359
'the sort of company…', *ibid*
'Nobody can be…', *ibid*

'made it highly...', *ibid*
56 'Answer to an invitation...', poem by WO'B, 1770, Add MSS 51361
    'this absolute refusal...', Ly SO'B's Journal, 1771, Add MSS 51359
57 'to obtain for Mr OB...', *ibid*
    'his affection was wholly...', *ibid*
    'from the profits...', *ibid*
58 'For I am weary...', cited in JH Jesse, *George Selwyn and His Contemporaries*, vol I, p. 20
    'an interesting story...', D Garrick to James Boswell, 17 Nov 1772, cited in Highfill et al, *A Biographical Dictionary...*, vol II, pp. 89-92
    'It was much hiss'd...', *ibid*
    'in the opinion...', Davies, *op. cit.*, p. 245
    'My Father was...', *The Duel*, Act II, Add MSS 51362
59 'hunting and shooting...', Ilchester, *Home of the Hollands*, p. 91
    'The house was always...', *ibid*
    'made our time pass...', Ly SO'B's Journal, 1774, Add MSS 51359
    'the first misfortune...', Ld Carlisle to George Selwyn, 14 Jan 1774, in Jesse, *op. cit.*, vol III, p. 67
60 'made them go...', Frances Greville to Fanny [Burney?], Monday [10 Jan 1771], Add MSS 51452
    'one thinks she had...', *ibid*
61 'The whole audience...', WO'B to Ste Fox, 8 Feb 1774, *ibid*
    'melancholy end', Ly SO'B's Journal, 1774, Add MSS 51359
62 'leaving their place...', Frances Greville to Ly Mary Fox, 28 Dec [1774], Add MSS 51452
    'It gave me great...', Frances Greville to Ly SO'B, 23 Apr 1764, Add MSS 51357
64 'very pretty spaniels...', Ly SB to Ly SO'B, 5 Nov 1776, Ilchester & Stavordale, *The Life and Letters of Lady Sarah Lennox*, vol I, p. 256
    'the place was...', Ly SO'B's Journal, 1775, Add MSS 51359
65 'make a provision...', *ibid*
    'the greater people...', *ibid*
    'do you remember...', Ly SB to Ly SO'B, 30 Dec 1777, Ilchester & Stavordale, *op. cit.*, vol I, p. 263
66 'I should certainly go...', ditto, 5 Nov 1776, *ibid*, pp. 255-256
    'tallied exactly with...', CJ Fox to WO'B, 15 Dec 1777, Add MSS 51467
67 'half dead with...', Ilchester & Stavordale, *op. cit.*, vol I, p. 257 (footnote drawn from Gen. Burgoyne's statement before the House of Commons)
    'Lady Acland's boat...', cited in Thorp (ed), *The Acland Journal*, p. xxvii
    'The most amiable...', *ibid*, p. xxvi
    'I do pity Lady...', Ly SB to Ly SO'B, 30 Dec 1777, Ilchester & Stavordale, *op. cit.*, vol I, p. 263
68 'every thing was...', Ly SO'B's Journal, 1779, Add MSS 51359
    'had he lived...', *ibid*

4. The Dye Is Cast

71 'I *must* give up...', WO'B to Ly SO'B, 31 Jan [1781], Add MSS 51352
    'did not like to...', Ly SO'B's Journal, 1781, Add MSS 51359
    'fagging all day...', WO'B to Ly SO'B, Monday night undated, Add MSS 51352
72 'You say I know...', Ly SL to Ly SO'B, 14 May 1781, Ilchester & Stavordale, *op. cit.*, vol II, pp. 8-10
    'there was a propriety...', Ly SO'B to Ly SL, 19 May 1781, *ibid*, pp. 11-13
73 'almost madness...', Ly SO'B's Journal, 1783, Add MSS 51359
    'He became tenacious...', *ibid*, 1784

'every thing I most...', *ibid*
74 'I am afraid you...', WO'B to Ly SO'B, 2 Aug 1784, Add MSS 51352
    'But in going...', Ly SO'B's Journal, Aug 1784, Add MSS 51359
    'many proofs of my...', *ibid*
75 'My Mother whose...', *ibid*, 1789
76 'I feel myself...', *ibid*
    'as unpleasant a one...', *ibid*, 1789
    '& even on the last...', *ibid*, 1792
77 'almost as dependant...', *ibid*
    — to be roughly brushed aside..., cited in Joanna Martin (ed), *The Penrice Letters 1768-1795*, p. 42
    'worthy the decline...', cited in TH White, *The Age of Scandal*, p. 90
    'lost eleven thousand...', *ibid*
    'had hurt his fortune...', Ly SO'B's Journal, Sept 1794, Add MSS 51359
78 'tho unable to assist...', *ibid*, June 1794
    'unexpected mark of...', *ibid*
    'a most bitter pill...', *ibid*, Apr 1797

Part 3: Darby and Joan

79 'The patient being...', Fearon, *A Treatise on Cancers*, cited in Hemlow et al (ed), *The Journals and Letters of Fanny Burney*, Vol vi, p. 209

5. A Dreadful Malady

80 'an advocate for...', Ly SO'B's Journal, 19 Oct 1798, Add MSS 51359
    'who has but one...', *ibid*
    'How foolish this...', *ibid*
81 'the longer I stay...', *ibid*, 1799
    'perform'd with safety...', *ibid*, 30 Mar 1799
    'All my ideas...', *ibid*
82 'yet I see he leans...', *ibid*, 5 Apr 1799
    'Lady Susan O'Brien's...', Ly SO'B to Charles Blicke, undated [Apr 1799], Add MSS 51357
    'that the Dread of...', Charles Blicke to Ly SO'B, 14 Apr 1799, *ibid*
    'like ordering one's own...', Ly SO'B's Journal, 19 Apr 1799, Add MSS 51359
83 'they look'd on him...', *ibid*, 21 Apr 1799
    'I am sure I feel...', *ibid*, 22 Apr 1799
    'with the greatest...', *ibid*, 1 May 1799
    '[A]s I had no idea...', *ibid*
    'Bright through the...', Fanny Burney to Esther Burney, 20 Sept 1811, Hemlow et al (eds), *The Journals and Letters of Fanny Burney*, Vol vi, p. 611
    'an odd mixture...', Harman, *Fanny Burney*, p. 306
    'I saw the glitter...', FB to EB, Hemlow et al, *op. cit.*, pp. 611-612
84 'When the wound was...', *ibid*, pp. 612-613
    'A kind of self...', Ly SO'B's Journal, 1 May 1799, Add MSS 51359
85 'great satisfaction it...', *ibid*, 29 May 1799
86 'all the good...', Ly SO'B's Journal, 3 June 1800, Add MSS 51359
    'He was the...', *ibid*
    'but no CF, no...', *ibid*, 29 May 1799
    'hoped that *no*...', CJ Fox to WO'B, 23 May 1799, Add MSS 51467
    'How shall I find...', Ly SN to Ly SO'B, undated [1799], Ilchester & Stavordale, *op. cit.*, vol II, p. 143
87 'as well as one...', Ly SO'B's Journal, 31 May 1799, Add MSS 51359

'the sight of him...', *ibid*, 8 Aug 1799
'I feel very...', *ibid*, Oct 1799
'Lady Susan may be...', Charles Blicke to WO'B, 3 Oct 1799, Add MSS 51358

6. Pandora's Box

88 'Mr OB reading to...', Ly SO'B's Journal, Feb 1800, Add MSS 51359
'Pandora's Box...', *ibid*, 14 May 1800
'for examining...', WM Pitt to WO'B, 13 May 1800, Add MSS 51358
'The secret of England's...', Fortescue, *History of the British Army*, vol iv, part 1, pp. 325 & 545-565

89 'lead to something...', WM Pitt to WO'B, 13 May 1800, Add MSS 51358
'I think we may...', Ly SO'B's Journal, 14 May 1800, Add MSS 51359
'It is some thing...', *ibid*, 5 June 1800

90 'this year another...', *ibid*, 18 July 1800
'I should be very...', Ld Ilchester to WO'B, 11 Aug 1800, Add MSS 51358
'do what pride...', Ly SO'B's Journal, 14 Aug 1800, Add MSS 51359

91 'at the end of my...', WO'B to Ld Ilchester, 18 Aug 1800, Add MSS 51358
'unwilling naturally to...', Ly SO'B's Journal, 14 Aug 1800, Add MSS 51359
'From the different...', Ly H Frampton to Ly SO'B, 2 Sept 1800, Add MSS 51357
'such is the world!...', Ly SO'B's Journal, Xmas 1800, Add MSS 51359

92 'The year and...', *ibid*, 1 Jan 1801
'Nothing is more...', *ibid*, Feb 1801
'grown fat & grey...', *ibid*, 1 Mar 1801
'It is extraordinary...', *ibid*, 11 Aug 1800

93 'the great readiness...', Prince William to WO'B, 1 June 1801, Add MSS 51352
'The idea that...', Ly SO'B's Journal, 24 July 1801, Add MSS 51359
'very low, &...', *ibid*, July 1802
'Melbury *again gone*...', *ibid*, 7 Sept 1802
'fear my poor...', *ibid*, 12 Sept 1802
'what will guardians...', 7 Sept 1802

94 'most kindly and...', *ibid*, Nov 1802
'try every court...', *ibid*, 21 Feb 1803
'I think I see such...', *ibid*, 7 July 1803
'I may say I...', *ibid*, 15 July 1803

95 '*no favorite*...', *ibid*, 11 Sept
'quite low, vex'd...', *ibid*, 23 Aug 1803
'he has not the...', *ibid*, 30 Dec 1803

96 'strange fate', *ibid*, 13 July 1804
'Admired by every...', *ibid*
'a most miserable...', Ly SN to Ly SO'B, 5 July 1804, Ilchester & Stavordale, *op. cit.*, vol II, pp. 162-163
'daily risk of losing...', ditto, 28 July 1804, *ibid*, p. 164
'well in health, but...', Ly SO'B to Ly E Feilding, 23 Aug 1804, TP
'he seems to me...', Ly SO'B's Journal, 6 Aug 1804, Add MSS 51359
'I can't say but...', Ly SO'B to Ly E Feilding, 23 Aug 1804, TP
'so many people...', Ly SO'B's Journal, 13 Aug 1804, Add MSS 51359

97 'For disagreeable...', WO'B to Ly SO'B, 21 Oct 1804, Add MSS 51352
'My poor Ly Sarah...', C Fox to Ly SO'B, 17 Oct 1804, Add MSS 51467
'my friends in...', WO'B to Ly SO'B, 17 Oct 1804, Add MSS 51352
'very ill indeed...', ditto, 21 Oct 1804, *ibid*
'too much discomposed...', Ly SO'B's Journal, 28 Nov 1804, Add MSS 51359
'My cheerfulness...', *ibid*, 2 Nov 1804

7. Trials of a Tax-Gatherer

98 'She is a great...', *ibid*, 25 Dec 1804
'I flatter'd myself...', *ibid*, 30 Dec 1804

99 'It is so desirable...', Ly SO'B's Journal, 29 Nov 1802, Add MSS 51359
'a return of giddyness...', *ibid*, 8 Aug 1803
'examine Rates & Taxes...', Ly SO'B to Ly E Talbot, 12 Dec [1802/3], TP
'he suffer'd the...', Ly SO'B's Journal, 13 Aug 1803, Add MSS 51359

100 'God forbid...', *ibid*, 23 Feb 1804
'*My Politicks* have...', *ibid*, 23 Jan 1806
'After the many...', *ibid*, 8 Feb 1806

101 'a very full, clear...', *ibid*, 30 Mar 1806
'so entirely out of...', *ibid*, 16 Sept 1806
'"I know Ly Susan..."', *ibid*, 23 Sept 1806
'Sic Transit Gloria...', *ibid*, 10 Oct 1806

102 'a fine day smiling...', *ibid*, 28 Feb 1808
'After the King...', *ibid*
'there cannot be room for...', *ibid*, 30 Dec 1806
'such a rushing in...', *ibid*, 16 July 1808

103 'Every day...', *ibid*, 5 Jan 1809
'Mr OB puzzled &...', Ly SO'B's Journal, 6 Jan 1807-15 May 1808, Add MSS 51359

104 'thinking & preparing...', *ibid*, 1 Oct 1809
'all sorts of attacks...', *ibid*, 9 Oct 1809
'a very *singular*...', *ibid*, 19 Nov 1809
'the proposal vexes...', *ibid*, 23 Nov 1809
'was thinking about...', *ibid*, 3 Aug 1811

105 'Mr O uneasy about...', *ibid*, 12 Nov 1810
'We go & settle...', Ly SO'B to Ly E Feilding, 24 Jan 1811, TP
'The letter say'd...', Ly SO'B's Journal, 3 Aug 1811, Add MSS 51359
'The whole transaction....', *ibid*, 13 Aug 1811

106 'To be hamper'd...', *ibid*
'I must tell you...', Ly SO'B to Ly E Feilding, 25 Oct 1811, TP
'tho without a...', Ly SO'B's Journal, 1 Dec 1811, Add MSS 51359

107 'tedious & disagreeable...', *ibid*, 6 Dec 1811
'hope as a true...', *ibid*, 31 Dec 1811
'I cannot conquer...', *ibid*, 31 Jan 1812
'quite a family one...', *ibid*, 13 Apr 1812
'*being at home*, her...', *ibid*

108 'Thus stands the...', *ibid*, 31 Dec 1812

109 'in a very tottering...', *ibid*, 26 June 1813
'the first summons...', *ibid*, 30 June 1813
'No cheerfulness now...', *ibid*, 3 Aug 1813
'Mr Floyer wishing...', *ibid*, 4 Aug 1813
'any man in his...', *ibid*, 7 Aug 1813
'rather die than go...', *ibid*, 29 Oct 1813

110 'I see my family...', *ibid*, 20 Sept 1813
'I feel it is only...', *ibid*, 29 Oct 1813
'*wrong*, my action...', *ibid*, 25 Dec 1813
'the trees beautiful...', *ibid*, 4 Jan 1814
'I can't help thinking...', *ibid*, 7 Jan 1814

111 'Few have struggled...', *ibid*, 7 Apr 1814

Sources

'I... found them...', Charlton Wollaston to Mary Frampton, undated [May 1814], cited in H Mundy (ed), *The Journal of Mary Frampton*, p. 176
'a good deal alter'd...', Ly SO'B's Journal, 16 May 1814, Add MSS 51360
'handsome but too...', *ibid*, 21 May 1814
'as unpleasant a...', *ibid*, 31 May 1814
'what will never...', *ibid*, 1 June 1814

112 'Illuminations, Cossacks, &c...', *ibid*, 3 June 1814
'I feel so...', *ibid*, 4 June 1814
'fell as if shot...', *ibid*, 25 June 1814
'drink a glass of...', *ibid*, 7 July 1814
'O always pleased...', *ibid*, 26 July 1814

113 'No great matter if...', *ibid*, 2 Oct 1814
'with a shortness of...', *ibid*, 21 Oct 1814
'My Lady recommended...', *ibid*, 22 Sept 1814
'still so ill as...', *ibid*, 1 Jan 1815

114 'not writing, &...', *ibid*, 14 Jan 1815
'She said he had...', *ibid*, 20 Jan 1815
'a letter from...' *ibid*, 23-31 Jan 1815
'most wonderfull...', *ibid*, 16 Mar 1815
'the first good...', *ibid*, 14 Mar 1815
'all war & misery...', *ibid*, 23 Mar 1815

115 'so little to animate...', *ibid*, 8 May 1815
'None sang — How often...', *ibid*, 20 May 1815
'to say how great...', *ibid*, 18 May 1815
'a compleat Victory...', *ibid*, 23 June 1815

116 'an hours walk with her...', *ibid*, 15 July 1815
'so fine, so sublime...', 28 July 1815
'they frighten &...', *ibid*, 29 July 1815

117 'always judging &...', *ibid*, 31 July 1815
'Older than any...', *ibid*
'after all the...', *ibid*, 5 Aug 1815
'I can tell you how...', Ly SO'B to Ly E Feilding, 14 Aug 1815, TP
'much alarm'd...', Ly SO'B's Journal, 30 Aug 1815, Add MSS 51360
'Cooper & Arden...', *ibid*, 31 Aug 1815

118 '*His* list of the last...', Add MSS 51352
'In my silence...', *ibid*

Part 4: Joan Alone

8. The Absent One

120 'Heaven grant...', Ly SO'B's Journal, 11 Sept 1815, Add MSS 51360
'Oh what a...', *ibid*
'I wish'd it should be...', *ibid*

121 'A Man Amiable...', *ibid*, 13 Sept 1815
'melancholy employment,' *ibid*, 15 Sept 1815
'silence & solitude...', *ibid*, 16 Sept 1815
'Nothing can be...', *ibid*, 19 Sept 1815
'a book of consolations...', *ibid*, 21 Sept 1815

122 'they are good...', *ibid*, 22 Sept 1815
'the separation seems...', *ibid*, 25 Sept 1815
'belov'd by...', *ibid*, 26 Sept 1815

LADY SUSAN'S UNSUITABLE MARRIAGE

'sad destitute...', *ibid*, 9 Oct 1815
'so near *him*...', *ibid*, 15 Oct 1815
'profess'd great kindness...', *ibid*, 6 Nov 1815
'still E in her usual...', *ibid*, 17 Nov 1815
123 'I don't know that...', *ibid*, 27 Nov 1815, Add MSS 51360
124 'the dear little Lord...', *ibid*, 8 Jan 1816
'It's a pleasure to...', *ibid*, 28 Feb 1816
125 'I feel my return to...', Ly SO'B to Ly E Feilding, 8 Mar 1816, TP
'& from those...', Ly SO'B's Journal, 10 Mar 1816, Add MSS 51360
126 'some beautiful verses...', *ibid*, 16 Apr 1816
127 'there was a propriety...', Ly SO'B to Ly SL, 19 May 1781, *ibid*, pp. 11-13

9. The Restoration of a Picture

128 'there can be no...', Ly SO'B's Journal, 1 Sept 1816, Add MSS 51360
'that day when...', *ibid*, 9 Sept 1816
'sailing on the...', Ly SO'B to Ly E Feilding, 14 Sept 1816, TP
'I did not think I...', Ly SO'B' Journal, 9 Sept 1816, Add MSS 51360
'Formerly, all my...', Benjamin Constant, *Adolphe*, translated by Carl Wildman, pp. 102-103
130 'nobody now asks...', Ly SO'B's Journal, 14 Sept 1816, Add MSS 51360
'It is again like...', *ibid*, 20 Sept 1816
'Glory of the...', *ibid*, 29 Sept 1816
'at the time...', *ibid*, 9 Dec 1816
'In very bad spirits...', *ibid*, 15 Feb 1817
131 'greatest favorite &...', *ibid*, 1 Mar 1817
'the loss of a valuable...', *ibid*, [early] May 1817
'much to any information...', *ibid*, 19 May 1817
'another week of...', *ibid*, 27 May 1817
'a great resource...', *ibid*, 5 June 1817
'can never do so...', *ibid*, 23 June 1817
'pleas'd the Floyers...', *ibid*, 2 Aug 1817
132 'no other person...', *ibid*, 1-4 Sept 1817
'I shall miss her...', *ibid*, 8 Sept 1817
'which he had destin'd...', *ibid*, 3 Apr 1816
'full of carriages &...', *ibid*, 15 Feb 1818
'with whom I may talk...', *ibid*, 12 Feb 1818
'I do not write...', Ly SO'B to Ly E Feilding, 25 Oct 1811, TP
'in interest or...', Ly SO'B's Journal, 5-6 Mar 1818, Add MSS 51360
'on her & my affairs...', *ibid*, 10 Mar 1818
133 'Had she met with...', *ibid*, 7 Apr 1818
'If he had married you...', *ibid*, 2 May 1818
'for heart, honor...', *ibid*
'very brilliant with...', *ibid*, 23 Apr 1818
the name of Gayest..., *ibid*, 24 Apr 1818
134 'there is a buoyancy...', *ibid*, 11 May 1818
'I am griev'd...', *ibid*, 14 May 1818
'tho fearfull of another...', *ibid*, 7 July 1818
'& in that room I...', *ibid*, 8, 9 & 10 July 1818

10. A Prodigy

135 'It's a cousin of...', Ly SO'B to Ly E Feilding, 6 Oct 1819, TP
136 'could know, approve or...', Ly SO'B's Journal, 25 Dec 1819, Add MSS 51360

      'disappointments...', *ibid*, 1 & 2 Sept 1819
      'I must either...', *ibid*, 5 Dec 1817
137 'very unpleasant...', *ibid*, 7 June 1821
      'pretty easy', *ibid*, 10 June 1821
      'threatening the loss...', *ibid*, 11 July 1821
      'who did not speak...', *ibid*, 18 July 1821
      'rather extraordinary...', *ibid*, 24 July 1821
138 'visibly afraid of...', *ibid*, 25 July 1821
      'all the securitys...', *ibid*, 12 Aug 1821
      'nothing but what...', *ibid*, 17 Aug 1821
      'to what avail...', *ibid*, 17 Oct 1821
      'he is not my...', *ibid*, 1 Nov 1821
139 'visiting for the last...', *ibid*, 31 Mar 1825
      'a greater decay of...', *ibid*, 3 May 1825
140 'the most liberal...', cited in Ilchester, *Home of the Hollands*, pp. 179-181
      'Sixty-two years had...', cited in Ilchester, *Chronicles of Holland House 1820-1900*, pp. 58-59
      'She is gone...', *ibid*, 27 Aug 1826
      'all the Talbots', *ibid*, 31 Dec 1826
      'I have plenty of...', *ibid*
141 'I pass'd the evening...', *ibid*, 13 June 1827
      'just large enough...', F Hardy, *The Early Life of Thomas Hardy*, p. 12
142 'They remained always...', Mundy (ed), *The Journal of Mary Frampton*, pp. 19-20

SELECT BIBLIOGRAPHY

Boswell, James, *London Journal 1762-1763* (London 2010)

Constant, Benjamin, *Adolphe and The Red Notebook* (New York 1959)

Cordingly, David, *Billy Ruffian: The Bellerophon and the Downfall of Napoleon* (London 2003)

Davies, Thomas, *Memoirs of the Life of David Garrick, Esq.* (London 1781)

Genest, John, *Some Account of the English Stage from the Restoration in 1660 to 1830* (London 1832)

Hardy, Florence Emily, *The Early Life of Thomas Hardy, 1841-1891* (London 1928)

Hardy, Thomas, *The Complete Poems* (London 1976)

Harman, Claire, *Fanny Burney: A Biography* (London 2000)

Hemlow, Joyce, et al (ed.), *The Journals and Letters of Fanny Burney (Madame D'Arblay)*, vol vi, France 1803-1812 (Oxford 1975)

Hibbert, Christopher, *Redcoats and Rebels: The War for America, 1770-1781* (London 1990)

Hibbert, Christopher, *George III: A Personal History* (London 1998)

Highfill, Philip H et al (eds), *A Biographical Dictionary of actors, actresses, musicians, dancers, managers and other stage personnel in London, 1660-1800* (Carbondale, Illinois, c.1973-c.1993)

Ilchester, Countess of, and Stavordale, Lord, *The Life and Letters of Lady Sarah Lennox* (London 1902)

Ilchester, 6th Earl of, *Henry Fox, First Lord Holland, His Family and Relations* (London 1920)
Ilchester, 6th Earl of, *The Home of the Hollands 1605-1820* (London 1937)
Ilchester, 6th Earl of, *Chronicles of Holland House 1820-1900* (London 1937)
Jesse, JH, *George Selwyn and His Contemporaries* (London 1843)
Lewis, WS, and Brown, Ralph S Jr (eds), *Horace Walpole's Correspondence with George Montagu*, vol 9 of the Yale edition of Horace Walpole's correspondence (London and New Haven 1941)
Little, David M, and Kahrl, George M (eds), *The Letters of David Garrick* (Oxford 1963)
Lynch, James L, *Box, Pit and Gallery: Stage and Society in Johnson's London* (California 1953)
Martin, Joanna, *The Penrice Letters, 1768-1795* (Swansea and Cardiff 1993)
Martin, Joanna, *A Governess in the Age of Jane Austen: The Journals and Letters of Agnes Porter* (London and Rio Grande, Ohio, 1998)
Martin, Joanna, *Wives and Daughters: Women and Children in the Georgian Country House* (London and New York 2004)
McCullough, David, *1776: America and Britain at War* (New York 2005)
Mereness, Newton D (ed), *Travels in the American Colonies* (New York 1916)
Mitchell, Leslie, *Holland House* (London 1980)
Mitchell, Leslie, *The Whig World, 1760-1837* (London and New York 2005)
Mitchell, LG, *Charles James Fox* (Oxford 1992)
Mundy, Harriot Georgiana (ed), *The Journal of Mary Frampton from the Year 1779 until the Year 1846* (London 1885)
Napier, Priscilla, *The Sword Dance: Lady Sarah Lennox and the Napiers* (London 1971)
O'Toole, Fintan, *A Traitor's Kiss: The Life of Richard Brinsley Sheridan* (London 1997)
O'Toole, Fintan, *White Savage: William Johnson and the Invention of America* (London 2005)
Peake, RB (ed), *Memoirs of the Colman Family* (London 1841)
Stone, George W Jr (ed), *The London Stage, 1660-1800* (Carbondale, Illinois, 1962)
Stone, George W Jr, and Kahrl, George M, *David Garrick: A Critical Biography* (Carbondale and Edwardsville, Illinois, 1979)
Stone, William L, *The Life and Times of Sir William Johnson, Bart* (Albany 1865)
Tillyard, Stella, *Aristocrats: Caroline, Emily, Louisa and Sarah Lennox, 1740-1832* (London 1994)
Thorp, Jennifer D (ed), *The Acland Journal: Lady Harriet Acland and the American War* (Winchester 1993)
Tomalin, Claire, *Thomas Hardy: The Time-Torn Man* (London 2006)
Walpole, Horace, *The Letters of Horace Walpole, Earl of Orford* (London 1846)
White, TH, *The Age of Scandal* (London 1950)
Wilcoxen, Charlotte, 'A Highborn Lady in Colonial New York', *New York Historical Society Quarterly* (Oct 1979)

Index

Page numbers in *italics* refer to illustrations

Abbotsbury 70, 76, 94, 106, 114, 128, 138
Acland, Henrietta (Harriot) *née* Fox-Strangways 54-5, 63, 66-8, 77, 81, 82-3, 85, 97, 103, 115, 116, 117
Acland, John Dyke 54, 66-8
Acland, Kitty 78
Acland, Sir Thomas 117
Addington, Henry, 1st Viscount Sidmouth 92, 99, 100
Adolphus, John 51
Albany 38, 50, 67
Alexander, William ('Lord Stirling') 31
Allen, John 139-40
Armistead, Elizabeth *see* Fox, Elizabeth *née* Armistead
Austen, Jane 73

Bankes, Mrs Henry (of Kingston Lacy), née Frances Woodley 133-4
Bath 96, 114, 131
Bentham, Jeremy 85 n.15
Blanco White, Joseph 139
Blicke, Charles 81, 82, 83, 84, 87
Boswell, James 28, 58
Boswell, Mr (W. O'Brien's deputy as Receiver-General for Taxes in Dorset) 99, 103-4, 105, 107, 108
Bristol Hot Wells 96
Browne, John Francis 99, 136-7, 138, 139
Brudenell, Rev. Edward 67
Brumpton, Mr 60-1
Bunbury, Sir Charles 48
Bunbury, Louisa 48, 72
Bunbury, Lady Sarah *née* Lennox 17, 20, 22, 24, 25, 31, 34, 41, 43, 44-8, 59, 64, 65-6, 67, 72-3, 78, 86, 92, 96-7, 111, 118, 127, 132-3, 135, 139, 140
Burgoyne, Major Gen. John 66-7
Burney, Fanny (Mme D'Arblay) 83-4, 85 n.15
Buxton 93
Byron, Lord George Gordon 119, 126, 133-4

Canajoharie 33, 39

Cary, Mrs 40-1
Cary, Major R. F. 40
Cathcart, Charles, 9th Lord Cathcart 18, 23
Charles II 18, 19
Charlotte of Mecklenburg-Strelitz, Queen 98
Clive, Lord Robert 28
Colden, Gov. Cadwallader 33, 39
Colman, George 42
Colman, George (The Elder) 58
Constant, Benjamin 128, 129 n.26
Cooper, Dr. Christopher 109, 117, 118
Cotes, Francis 34, *129*, 132, 134
Covent Garden 20 n.2, 22, 42, 58
Cowper, William 97
Crabbe, George 126
Crewe, Frances Anne 133
Croghan, Col. George 32-3

Damer, Mrs Lionel 77, 111
Davies, Thomas 21, 58
de Kerouaille, Louise, Duchess Portsmouth 19
DeLancey, Oliver 31
Digby, Charlotte *née* Fox 25, 27, 55
Digby, Charlotte *née* Gunning 85 n.15
Digby, Edward 25 n.4
Digby, Lady Lucy *née* Fox-Strangways 81, 85 n.15
Digby, Col. Stephen 80-1, 82, 85-6
Discove 75, 76, 96
Drummond, Adam 28-9, 30, 31, 32
Drury Lane 8, 9, 17, 20, 21, 22, 24, 29, 42, 57, 58, 60, 63
Dundas, Henry 88

Ellis, Wellbore 37

Farquhar, George 20, 21
Farquhar, Sir Walter 81, 83
Fearon, Henry 79
Feilding, Capt. Charles 123, 140
Feilding, Lady Elizabeth (Talbot) *see* Fox-Strangways, Lady Elizabeth Theresa (Eliza)
Fitzgerald, Emily *née* Lennox, Duchess of Leinster 19
Fitzgerald, James, 20th Earl Leinster 19

– 157 –

Fitzpatrick, Lady Mary *see* Fox, Lady Mary *née* Fitzpatrick
Floyer, Rev. William 90, 91, 94, 109, 110, 113, 114, 118, 120, 121, 128, 135, 136
Floyer, Mrs 115, 136
Floyer, William 136
Foote, Samuel 21, 30, 41-2
Fort Johnson 39
Fortescue, Sir John 88
Fox, Caroline 59, 85 n.15, 86, 101, 139
Fox, Lady Caroline *née* Lennox, Lady Holland 19, 24, 46, 49, 51, 55, 56, 61
Fox, Charles James 19, 22, 23, 24, 47, 57, 59, 65, 66, 69, 71, 73, 77, 86, 88, 92, 96, 100, 101, 111, 131, 133
Fox, Elizabeth *née* Armistead 86
Fox, Henry, 1st Lord Holland 17, 18-19, 23, 24-6, 27, 28-9, 31, 32, 33, 34, 35-7, 39, 40, 42, 43, 44, 45, 46-8, 49, 51, 55, 56-7, 59, 61, 125, 133
Fox, Gen. Henry Edward 46 n.8, 86
Fox, Henry Richard, 3rd Lord Holland 60, 61, 63, 139-40
Fox, Lady Mary *née* Fitzpatrick 44-5, 59-60, 61, 62-3
Fox, Sir Stephen 18, 19-20
Fox, Stephen (Ste), 2nd Lord Holland 19, 44, 46-7, 59-60, 61, 62, 77, 86
Fox-Strangways, Caroline Leonora *née* Murray, Lady Ilchester 106, 107-8, 110, 121, 122, 124, 136
Fox-Strangways, Hon. Rev. Charles Redlynch 7, 131, 136, 137, 138, 139, 141
Fox-Strangways, Charlotte Anne 95
Fox-Strangways, Elizabeth *née* Horner, Lady Ilchester 7, 19, 24, 30, 35, 43, 44, 45, 46, 47, 48, 49, 50, 55, 56, 63, 64, 65, 67-8, 74, 75-6
Fox-Strangways, Lady Elizabeth Theresa (Eliza) 22, 77, 96, 99, 105, 106, 114, 115, 117, 122-4, 125, 128, 129, 130, 132, 133, 135, 139, 140
Fox-Strangways, Harriot *see* Acland, Harriot *née* Fox-Strangways
Fox-Strangways, Henry (Harry) Stephen, 3rd Earl Ilchester 94, 95, 98, 102, 106, 107, 111, 121, 122, 124, 130, 131, 136, 141
Fox-Strangways, Henry Thomas, 2nd Earl Ilchester 71, 74, 77, 78, 80, 82, 85, 90-1, 93-4, 123, 133
Fox-Strangways, Henry Thomas Leopold, Lord Stavordale 124
Fox-Strangways, Louisa Emma 95, 103, 113, 133, 139
Fox-Strangways, Maria *née* Digby, Lady Ilchester 80, 91, 93-5, 98, 102-3, 107, 114

Fox-Strangways, Maria Theresa *née* Grady, Lady Ilchester 93
Fox-Strangways, Stephen, 1st Earl Ilchester 7, 17-18, 19, 24, 25, 26, 30, 34, 35, 36, 43, 44, 46, 54, 57, 65, 116
Fox-Strangways, Col. Stephen Strangways Digby 66, 93, 95, 102, 116, 117, 123
Fox-Strangways, Susan 131
Fox-Strangways, Brig.-Gen. Tom 115-16
Frampton, Lady Harriot *née* Fox-Strangways 91, 99, 103, 121, 137, 138, 139, 141
Frampton, James 99, 104, 108, 137, 138
Frampton, Mary 111, 141-2

Gage, Gen. Thomas 40
Garrick, David 17, 20, 21, 22, 28, 31, 41-2, 44, 56, 58
Garrick, George 30, 42
Gates, Gen. Horatio 67
Genest, John 21, 26
George II 18
George III 20, 66, 67 n.12, 77, 89, 92, 98, 133
Gordon, Lord Adam 31, 38, 39, 43
Gordon, Lord William 48
Grenville, George 38
Greville, Frances 60, 62-3
Greville, Fulke 60

Haiti (St Domingo) 88-9, 92-3, 94
Hardy, Florence *née* Dugdale 7
Hardy, Jemima 7
Hardy, Thomas (1778-1837) 7-8
Hardy, Thomas (1811-92) 7-8
Hardy, Thomas (1840-1928) 7-8, 9, 64, 75, 112 n.21
Harman, Claire 83, 85 n.15
Hawkins, Adair 80, 81, 83, 87
Herbert, Henry, 10th Earl Pembroke 60-1
Hervey, John, 2nd Baron 18, 19
Hobson, Mrs 80-1
Hodges, Walter Parry 104-5, 106-7, 136-8
Holland House 22, 23, 32, 47, 48, 55, 62, 63, 135, 139-40
Horner, Susanna *née* Strangways 24
Horner, Thomas Strangways 24
Howard, Frederick, 5th Earl Carlisle 59-60
Hume, Joseph 137, 138

Johnson, Sir William 33, 38, 39, 43
Jones, Inigo 17

Kenton Green 56, 59
Killerton House 54, 116
Kingston Maurward 88, 110

INDEX

Lansdowne House 133
Lansdowne, Lady Louisa *see* Fox-Strangways, Louisa Emma
Larrey, Dominique-Jean 83
Lennox, Caroline *see* Fox, Lady Caroline
Lennox, Charles, 2nd Duke Richmond 19, 45
Lennox, Emily *see* Fitzgerald, Emily, Duchess Leinster
Lennox, Sarah *see* Bunbury, Lady Sarah *née* Lennox
Louis XVIII 114

Maiden Newton 7, 52
Manners, John, Marquis of Granby 42
Marsham, Sophia, *née* Pitt, Countess of Romney 109
Melbury House 19, 32, *52*, 63, 67, 70, 73, 76, 93, 94, 96-7, 102, 106, 110, 121, 122, 124, 131, 137, 140
Melbury Osmond 7
Mohawk River 29, 33, 34, 38-9
Montagu, George 17
Moore, Sir Henry 40
Murphy, Arthur 21
Murray, Rev. Edward 7
Murray, James 43

Napier, Charles James 72 n.13
Napier, Col. George 72, 78, 92, 96-7
Napier, Louisa 96, 97
Napier, Sarah *see* Bunbury, Lady Sarah *née* Lennox
Napoleon Bonaparte 83, 110, 114, 115, 117, 129 n.26
New York 31-3, 35, 37-8, 40, 42, 45, 48, 50
Niagara Falls 43
North, Lord Frederick 57, 65, 67 n.12

O'Brien, William 7, 8-9, 15-16, 17, 18, 20-1, 23, 25, 26-51, 54, 55, 56, 57-8, 60, 63, 64, 65, 66, 69-76, 80, 82, 87, 88-92, 94, 97-118, 120-1, 122, 123, 125-7, 128, *129*, 132, 133, 134, 136, 137, 140-1, *142*

Pattison, Mr (Banker) 105, 107, 108, 118, 138
Penrice 105, 106
Petty, Lord Henry, 5th Marquess of Lansdowne 101, 103
Pitt, Grace-Amelia *née* Seymer 135-6
Pitt, Margaret 109-10, 112-13, 116, 117, 121, 135
Pitt, William (The Younger) 65, 88, 92, 100, 101, 111
Pitt, William Morton 65, 88-9, 99, 101, 104, 105, 108, 109, 112-13, 114, 121, 135-6, 137

Read, Katherine 17, 18, 23, 96
Redlynch 19, 22, 23, *52*, 53, 60, 74, 75, 96
Reynolds, Joshua 22
Roberts, Lieut. Benjamin 43
Robertson, Col. James 32
Rowe, Nicholas 17
Russell, Lord John 139
Russell, Lord William 139

Saratoga 66, 67 n.12
Scott, Sir Walter 115
Selkirk, Alexander 114
Selwyn, George 57-8, 59, 60
Selwyn, Rev. Townshend 134
Seymour-Conway, Francis, 1st Earl Hertford, 17, 18
Stinsford Church 7, 63, 90, 111, 120, 127, 134, 141, *142*
Stinsford Farm 65, 78, 90
Stinsford House 7, 8, 63-5, 70, 73, 75, 77, 87, 88, 89, 90-1, 93, 94-5, 97, 98, 108, 109, 111-12, 115-116, 117, 121, 124, 125, 126, 130, 134

Talbot, Lady Mary Lucy *née* Fox Strangways 77, 105, 112, 131, 133, 140
Talbot, Thomas Mansel 105
Talbot, William Davenport 123
Talbot, William Henry Fox 114, 138, 140
Touchet, Samuel 28-9, 34-5, 36, 37-8, 42, 44, 49, 50, 56

Upton, Clotworthy (Tatty) Lord Templeton 28, 30, 34, 36, 40, 45

Walpole, Horace 8, 17, 18, 19, 20, 51, 77
Walpole, Sir Robert 18
Watts, John 31, 32, 39
Westminster Abbey 101, 111
Weymouth 70, 77
Wightwick, Miss 118, 120, 131-2
William Frederick (Prince), Duke Gloucester and Edinburgh 92-3
William Henry (Prince), 1st Duke Gloucester 20, 92
Williams, Sir Charles Hanbury 139
Wilton House 60
Winterslow House 59, 60, 61, 62
Wollaston, Charlton Byam 108, 109, 111, 138
Woodward, Henry 20

Young, Edward 23